MILITARY INDUSTRIALIZATION
AND ECONOMIC DEVELOPMENT

UNIDIR

United Nations Institute for Disarmament Research

UNIDIR is an autonomous institution within the framework of the United Nations. It was established in 1980 by the General Assembly for the purpose of undertaking independent research on disarmament and related problems, particularly international security issues.

The work of the Institute aims at:

1. Providing the international community with more diversified and complete data on problems relating to international security, the armaments race, and disarmament in all fields, particularly in the nuclear field, so as to facilitate progress, through negotiations, towards greater security for all States and toward the economic and social development of all peoples;

2. Promoting informed participation by all States in disarmament efforts;

3. Assisting ongoing negotiations in disarmament and continuing efforts to ensure greater international security at a progressively lower level of armaments, particularly nuclear armaments, by means of objective and factual studies and analyses;

4. Carrying out more in-depth, forward-looking, and long-term research on disarmament, so as to provide a general insight into the problems involved, and stimulating new initiatives for new negotiations.

The contents of UNIDIR publications are the responsibility of the authors and not of UNIDIR. Although UNIDIR takes no position on the views and conclusions expressed by the authors of its research reports, it does assume responsibility for determining whether they merit publication.

UNIDIR

Palais des Nations
CH-1211 Geneva 10
Tel. (022) 734 60 11
Fax (022) 733 98 79

Military Industrialization and Economic Development: Theory and Historical Case Studies

Raimo Väyrynen

UNIDIR
United Nations Institute for Disarmament Research

Dartmouth
Aldershot · Brookfield USA · Hong Kong · Singapore · Sydney

© United Nations Institute for Disarmament Research 1992

Published by
Dartmouth Publishing Company Limited
Gower House
Croft Road
Aldershot
Hants GU11 3HR
England

Dartmouth Publishing Company Limited
Distributed in the United States by
Ashgate Publishing Company
Old Post Road
Brookfield
Vermont 05036
USA

A CIP catalogue record for this book is available from the British Library and the US Library of Congress.

ISBN 1 85521 286 2

Printed in Great Britain at the University Press, Cambridge

Contents

Preface

Following the International Conference on the Relationship between Disarmament and Development held in the United Nations, New York, from 24 August - 11 September 1987, UNIDIR undertook to execute several aspects of the Action Programme in the Final Document adopted by the Conference. To this end specific research projects were formulated to analyze the economic and social consequences of military expenditure, to focus on the disarmament-development perspective, to promote collective knowledge of the non-military threats to international security and to examine issues related to the conversion of military industry to civilian production.

Professor Raimo Väyrynen's research report is one of such research projects the funding of which was made possible through a grant by the Government of Finland. I take this opportunity of expressing UNIDIR's gratitude for this. The author probes the facile assumption that military industrialization has "spin off" benefits for economic development and examines the linkage between military and civilian industries. He looks at specific case studies - Japan 1868-1914; Britain 1897-1914; Brazil 1960-90 and USA 1960-90 and argues the thesis that military industrialization often - and not always - has detrimental economic consequences but that other variables such as a country's general economic performance and its relationship to the global economic environment are also important. The relationship between military industrialization and economic development is clearly a complex one and this research report explores its various nuances.

I would like to thank Professor Raimo Väyrynen for his patient scholarship. Anita Blétry prepared this manuscript for publication. The views expressed in this publication are not necessarily those of UNIDIR. I have no doubt however that the publication is an important and timely contribution to the ongoing discussion on the rationale for high military expenditure especially in the present post Cold War international situation.

Jayantha Dhanapala
Director

Chapter 1
Science, Technology and the Arms Race

Technology: Civilian and Military

The basic function of technology, broadly understood, is to make potential resources real in order to enable their application in economy and society. Technology can help in processing natural resources, improving production processes and facilitating different forms of communication. Its development is accompanied with the need for a better-educated and sophisticated labour force. In effect, technology and organization combine productive inputs into novel applications. In that way technology has been an essential ingredient in the movement from extensive to intensive economic activities and from an undifferentiated society to a deeper socio-economic division of labour. In other words, technological progress has been associated with complexity and pluralism.

There are basically two ways of looking at the historical development of technology. It may be considered either as a relatively autonomous, self-steering process or an inseparable element in the broader transformation of socio-economic systems (Cox 1987, pp. 313-14). The concept of "technological trajectories" suggests that technological innovations have self-steering properties within a paradigm. In this approach, "technological paradigm" refers to a mutually compatible pattern of technologies, policies and productive organization which is often associated with an emerging industry. The pattern is obviously different in decaying industries; the paradigm may differ thus from one "technological regime" to another (Nelson and Winter 1977; Dosi 1982). Machine-tool and transistor technologies are both examples of a coherent paradigm in which technology, policy and organization have interacted with each other.

The choice between these two approaches, that is, the autonomy of technology and the interdependence of technology and society, is difficult and perhaps unnecessary. I am inclined to stress the autonomous aspects of technological development, in that it converts scientific research into an economic and social force. The utility of technology can be seen in the efforts of various political and organizational forces to appropriate it to serve their own purposes. However, none of them can appropriate technology alone as long as the scientific establishment has a degree of independence; if that independence is destroyed the progress of science and technology stagnates.

In a sense there is a struggle for technology, especially its most advanced variants, in every society. Both the market forces and public organizations are interested in searching, sponsoring and utilizing specific sets of technologies for their own purposes. The reasons for rivalry are quite self-evident; technology and, one might add, information is pivotal in the race for competitive national and corporate advantage. The competition is mitigated, however, by the fact that it is not necessarily generalized; technological resources are a general productive force, but they also yield specific applications. There is simultaneously a strong common interest to strengthen the technological basis of society in general and a competition for the specific applications. Even then, strategic alliances to develop and utilize technology are quite common, especially between major corporations, but also across the private/public divide.

These remarks pertain also to the distinction between civilian and military technologies, which have a common basis in the scientific establishment of the country and have a measure of common uses, but which are also differentiated by their specific applications. This means that the civilian and military technological regimes are supposed to have some intrinsic properties that distinguish them from each other, primarily because the specific user interests pose different requirements to civilian and military technologies.

In the capitalist world the properties of civilian technology are shaped in the first place by the demand in the national and, increasingly, in the transnational markets. Technological development is not principally intended to build up national forces of production, but to promote the competitive advantage of corporations or their alliances. That is why the emphasis is on the strong links between research institutions and industry based on research contracts, the development of commercially relevant technologies and the establishment of specific mechanisms to disseminate and utilize research results. The speed of innovations and the efficiency of their commercial utilization are the decisive factors in determining the role of science and technology in the market (Porter 1990, pp. 630-37).

Advanced technologies are increasingly controlled by major transnational corporations for whom they are also instruments of competition; a grip on leading technologies is vital for the attainment and maintenance of an edge in the market. Such an edge erodes easily, however: "if technological advantage is one of the most effective means through which the large firm maintains power it is also one of the most fragile. The threat of obsolescence continually jeopardises its power base". These facts explain why the leading companies have a genuine interest both in developing new technologies and in protecting them against the dangers of competition (Bertin and Wyatt 1988, pp. 10-11).

Usually, the growing costs of R&D necessitate the pursuit of cost-sharing and the expansion of the economies of scale. That is why the companies feel the pressure to expand to the world market and to conclude strategic alliances. In turn this leads to the diffusion of technology through the market to other corporations, if its transfer is not limited by a variety of restrictive practices. Such a diffusion is not necessarily harmful, and it might even be useful, for example, for cost-sharing purposes, to involve active rivals in co-operative R&D projects (Porter 1990, pp. 636-37).

The requirements of military technology are defined by the military organization with a view to its employment in warfare with the enemy. The performance of weapons thus becomes the overriding criterion in their development. In that sense the development of military technology is dictated by the external demands of political and military necessity. In that context it is argued that technological innovations are needed to achieve or preserve the military edge and the ensuing political leverage in interstate rivalries. These qualifications loom larger in political decision than the internal considerations, that is, the economic and social viability of the technologies in question (Thomas 1990, 826-8, 833-5).

The performance criteria of weapons are supposed to be best satisfied by the centralized decision-making and the modern manufacturing methods (Noble 1987, pp. 330-4). While the development of technology in the market is decentralized between corporations, the military industrialization is associated with the centralized control of the economy that can be achieved by the state intervention. The centralization tends to lead to the political protection of key technologies whose control is needed if the state wants to pursue the strategy of "keep ahead mercantilism" (Gill and Law 1988, p. 112). Too strong a reliance on such a strategy may become costly, however.

Edvard Kolodziej (1987, pp. 305-7) has pointed out that even though the strategic political incentives may be decisive in launching the arms industries, the economic and technological constraints of sustaining indigenous production assume, over time, an independent character. For example, the need to cover the mounting costs of development and production and to limit the balance of payment deficits fosters the expansion of both the manufacturing and export of arms (Väyrynen 1978). The domestic cost pressures push towards the international dissemination of weapons and weapons technologies. Thus, the internal requirements of the arms industry and the strategy of "keep ahead mercantilism" clash with each other.

The strategic mercantilism may try to rely entirely on domestic resources, to build on them an indigenous arms industry and to recoup the expenses by an active export policy. India tried this policy, but its indigenous projects, focusing on the aircraft industry, largely failed. Since the 1960s India has extensively relied on the licensed production of Soviet and West European weapons systems. As India has domestic political restraints on arms exports, its military industries have become costly for the national economy to bear (Gupta 1990). Brazil provides a different example in that it has been more active in exporting the products of its military industry than India, for example.

Another variant of the strategic mercantilism blocks the export of key military technologies in order to prevent the adversaries from benefiting from them. This variant is appropriate only for relatively large industrialized countries, since they have sufficient resources to engage in it. The protection of nationally developed technologies is a double-edged sword, however. It is often criticized as short-sighted because it undermines the commercial uses of technologies and deprives them of the impetus derived from the competition in the market. In that way strategic mercantilism probably contributes to the relative economic decline. The debates in the United States and Western Europe on the balance of military advantages and commercial disadavantages of the COCOM embargo against the Socialist countries well illustrate the dilemma (Cyert and Mowery 1989, pp. 34-5; Chesnais et al. 1990, pp. 76-9; Lucas 1990, pp. 145-76).

Strategic mercantilism may be wrong in that it supposes the effects of the international dissemination of military technologies to be necessarily harmful for the nation's relative position. However, the international diffusion of military technologies may foster their qualitative improvement at home and in that way enhance the nation's military standing. The spread of advanced technologies encourages the allocation of funds to military R&D because only by keeping ahead can the leading countries maintain their relative security and power position. As a consequence, in the leading powers there is a mutual process of reinforcement between the technological arms race and its international spread (Buzan 1987, pp. 36-9).

This phenomenon results, however, in the burgeoning economic costs and the growing political and military instability of international relations. The resources absorbed by the technological arms race are deprived from the civilian sector unless the spin-off process operates effectively between the sectors. This may lead, in turn, to the decline in the nation's relative economic position. In that sense the international spread of military technologies may have an indirect negative impact on the economic development of the exporting country.

The international dissemination of weapon technologies should be looked at also from the recipient's perspective. The importation of arms and military technology obviously increases military capability, but hardly contributes in an unequivocal manner to the economic and technological progress (Deger and Sen 1987). Nor do the weak linkages between civilian and military industries, limited job creation and the strains on the foreign exchange reserves recommend the establishment of large-scale systems of arms manufacturing (Ball 1988, pp. 357-82). To avoid the adverse economic effects of arms production it may be better to obtain the weapons from the patron state than to produce them oneself (Mullins 1987, p. 90). This suggestion can be contested by the argument that, at least in the short and middle run, there are marginal gains from the investment in arms production, and, if not real economic and technological gains, at least a perception of their existence (Kolodziej 1987, pp. 331-2).

The civilian and military user interests converge in the emphasis on vigorous basic research, which is considered a key to both civilian and military technology; without advanced scientific research there hardly can be innovations in military technology (Garden 1989, pp. 134-5). Yet the market-based and state-based user interests may also differ and even contradict each other. "For national security reasons states may wish to monopolise particular military-industrial technologies, but the economies of technological innovation drive them to policies which facilitate diffusion" (Gill and Law 1987, p. 78).

Civilian and military user interests may differ in other respects. For example, their differences may give rise to trade-offs in the innovation process. Military technologies may be so specialized that civilian applications are difficult to develop. This limits the economies of scale in the military R&D and may even lead to diseconomies (Deutsch and Schöpp 1987, pp. 338-9; Kubbig 1986, pp. 213-14). The problem is not only the excessive specification of military products at the advanced end of the technology continuum. The overspecification may also concern quite ordinary non-military equipment produced for the military (Weida and Gertcher 1986, pp. 139-40).

Thus, it would be simplistic to conclude that the military/non-military divide provides the sole key to explain overspecification and other problems in the application of technology. Furthermore, the incompatibility between civilian and military interests is by no means total. While being conceptually distinct, the civilian and military design criteria and organization may overlap or be otherwise connected. In effect, one may speak of three different types of technologies: pure civilian technologies, pure military technologies and mixed civilian-military technologies. Obviously, pure civilian technologies and mixed civilian-military technologies dominate the scene.

Both civilian and military technologies have their specific determinants which can be regarded as co-ordinates of technological spaces that include both real, potential and imaginary technologies to be used to solve specific problems (Egziabher 1982). In addition to having their separate spheres, civilian and military technological spaces also overlap with each other. This overlapping region is "where synergism of military and civilian criteria takes place". From the standpoint of rapid technical innovation it would be best to focus on "technologies that fall in the central region. Technology possessing criteria in this synergistic region will have the benefit from both military and civilian interests, funding and progress" (Shaw 1987, pp. 246-7).

What are, then, the criteria common to both the civilian and military technological spaces? Such criteria must be formulated in terms that are sufficiently general to capture features beyond the specific technical characteristics of different technologies. In Shaw's (1987, pp. 250-3) view the criteria could include centralization, transportation, communication, standardization, subordination and the removal of human intervention.

Centralization contributes both to the command of military operations and to the achievement of the economies of scale. Transportation facilitates military mobility and creates a distribution network for civilian goods, while communication helps to co-ordinate both military and business operations. Standardization is a means to homogenize and integrate the non-human elements of a centralized organization, whether military or civilian, while subordination performs the same task for the human elements. Behind these factors is the idea of a perfect military organization that would function without frictions and breakdowns and that could be transplanted in the civilian system of production as well.

In order to make the ideal centralized and standardized system work without frictions, the human element should be removed as far as possible. In this effort, "ultimately what is involved is nothing less than an attempt to insulate the system from uncertainty by creating a perfectly controlled and perfectly stable . . . artificial world. Thus the ideas which underlay technology . . . might be summed up as a one-to-one link between cause and effect, repetitiveness, specialization, integration, certainty, and finally efficiency" (van Creveld 1989, p. 315). A similar view informs the so-called scientific strategy. In such a strategy the military force is regarded as directed instrumental capability which can be rationally controlled to achieve desired ends (Reynolds 1989, pp. 87-8).

A perfect technological and strategic system does not permit the intervention of the human factor. In reality, the underlying logic of war is, however, much different from the logic of technology; it is unpredictable rather than controllable, configurative rather than linear in terms of its causality. The logic of war and of technology not only differ, but they can be opposite to each other (van Creveld 1989, pp. 316-20). The Clausewitzian logic of war worked in technologically rather simple circumstances, but the increasing complexity, versatility and destructiveness of technology has undermined the credibility and efficiency of this logic.

This questions the real political and military significance of such notions as technological superiority. It may be relevant in the peacetime comparisons of military capabilities as the perception of differences, and its political consequences matter. However, it is doubtful whether such a superiority is as important in war where the frictions and outright failures complicate its utilization. Ultimately, technological superiority is tested in war, in which its perception becomes an academic issue and only its military impact becomes decisive.

Civilian and military technologies overlap, but there are also spaces in which they do not interact at all. That is why these spaces have their own independent impact on the development of society. Most theories of technological innovation deal exclusively with its civilian aspects. They usually postulate a positive association between the transformation of the market by such innovations and the economic development. Technological innovations spread through competition and force the social and productive organizations of individual countries to adapt to them in order to remain capable of economic growth. In that way technological innovations foster structural homogeneity, but do not dictate it: "different ideological and social forms may be devised as consistent with a given technology" (Cox 1987, p. 313).

Theories concerning the military origins of economic development are much less common, but by no means non-existent. Gautam Sen (1984, pp. 7-8) has argued that "at the bottom the motivation for rapid industrial change is almost invariably of a military nature. Other factors like the desire for economic autonomy are important . . . but even economic insecurity ultimately stems from the underlying militarization of international political relations". This approach suggests that in competitive international relations economic development is made possible not so much by the market as by state intervention. In other words, self-sufficient domestic industries should be established both to sponsor civilian and military production capabilities (Gill and Law 1987; Jones 1988, pp. 159-63).

The importance of military origins of economic development has not only been stressed in the tradition of national economic realism, but also in a world-market perspective. In this vein it has been argued that "technologies supporting a world-market economy . . . derive as much from military goals as from commercial forces" (Shaw 1987, p. 253). This argument makes sense in the way that global communication systems often have military origins. In a broader sense it is somewhat difficult to comprehend, however. The stress on national security and military capabilities mean that "transnational corporations are denied equal access and treatment compared with national firms" (Gill and Law 1989, p. 493).

For the purposes of this study, the overlapping region of the civilian and military technological spaces is the most pertinent one. In this cross-section these two types of technologies can interact in three different ways. First, civilian and military technologies can experience parallel progress under a variety of influences, in particular the overall industrial advance. This may have been in Thorstein Veblen's mind when he suggested that the "mechanistic logic" of industrialism transforms both the civilian and military life, perhaps in this temporal order. That is why the "logic of warfare too has become to be the same mechanistic logic that makes the modern state of the industrial arts" (Veblen 1917, pp. 306-10).

Obviously, overlapping civilian and military technologies interact in reality more closely than the idea of parallel progress suggests. The other alternatives focus, then, on the nature and direction of causality between civilian amd military innovations. The causality may originate either from the military or civilian sources and operates in reality in the overlapping region of military and civilian technologies. This region is primarily composed of dual-purpose technologies, such as nuclear and chemical industries and lasers, that have potential both for economic development and military destruction (Dolman 1981).

Linkages Between Civilian and Military Technologies

To facilitate discussion of the linkages between civilian and military technologies one can make a distinction between the spin-off and spin-on effects (Dower 1989). The spin-off effect is directed from military R&D and production to the civilian industries; the military power also creates economic wealth. The spin-off effect is both a descriptive and a normative concept. In addition to depicting a potential empirical relationship it is also used to justify military production not only by the nation's security needs, but also by its contribution to economic development. The examples of jet engines, computers and nuclear power plants suggest that the military interests attached to new technologies may considerably accelerate and direct their development.

The spin-on effect operates in the reverse direction; the advance of civilian technologies facilitates new military applications. The spin-on effect may be observed both at the macro- and the micro-level. The macro-level interpretation of the spin-on effect states that extensive and advanced technological and economic resources are needed, first, to develop the system of military technology and, secondly, to allocate sufficient human and other capital to launch and sustain the military projects. On the other hand, the micro-interpretation focuses on the spin-on processes from the specific civilian technologies, initially developed for the market, to new military applications.

This distinction is related to a difference between tangible and intangible spin-ons and spin-offs. The tangible spin-offs are derived from the direct transfer to commercial uses of specific products, processes or materials developed in the military sphere. The intangible spin-offs are created by the indirect contribution of military-industrial knowledge to commercial operations by the transfer of technical innovations, organizational solutions and managerial techniques. The existence of intangible spin-offs, together with the scarcity of relevant data and the inadequacy of military R&D indicators, shows how difficult it is to assess the real economic impact of military industrialization (Kubbig 1986, pp. 200-3).

The spin-off phenomenon is akin to the standard conception of multiplier effects, but is not usually related to them as its analysis tends to ignore the connections with investment and employment. Rather the spin-off concept is used to refer to the transfer of specific technical innovations from the military to the civilian sphere. The basic idea behind this concept is that an invention made for military purposes is converted to a civilian application which is subsequently produced for the commercial market (Trebilcock 1969, pp. 475-6).

This means that the spin-off concept is geared to specific technologies and products. Its scope may be expanded, however, beyond the technical aspects: "Spin-offs can be defined as a transfer of technology from the area where it is developed to other areas. This may take the form of products, processes, organizational techniques, or knowledge" (Christensen 1989, p. 21). In other words, spin-offs include also the organizational experiences and knowledge gained in the military production which are often overlooked in the relevant literature.

The concept of spin-off suggests that there is a mutually supportive relationship between the civilian and military technologies and, in particular, that military R&D and production turn out civilian applications. The contrary argument is that the dependence of the civilian economy on the military technology may develop into a trade-off in the development of national economies. Indeed, the spin-off processes materialize usually within national economies and seldom assume a transnational dimension.

One of the exceptions is the Strategic Defence Initiative (SDI) programme, a major technological undertaking as such, to which the Reagan Administration recruited allied governments and companies from Europe and Japan. The SDI programme was supposed both to utilize the technological resources of Germany and Japan in particular and simultaneously to give an impetus to their further development. In reality, the governments and companies involved were deeply concerned with the distribution of relative gains and costs. In most cases, the German companies have been disappointed with the distribution of gains and restrictions placed on the transfer of technology in the SDI co-operation (Daalder 1987, pp. 67-98; Kubbig 1988, pp. 21-6).

In a more general vein, it has been suggested that the investments of major powers in the development of advanced military technologies have major adverse effects on the developing nations. In terms of the global allocation of resources this is no doubt the case; the spending on weapons systems reduces the possibilities for using the resources for alternative civilian purposes. The global economic effects of military programmes are, however, often indirect and complex and for this reason difficult to trace. That is why they are difficult to attribute to specific actors and projects (Hoag 1987; Brzoska and Lock 1988).

In the micro-context the negative spin-off operates when a specific product or process transferred from the military sphere is so uncompetitive by its price or technical character that it survives in the market only by the support of the government. In the macro-context the trade-off appears when the extensive allocation of resources for military purposes weakens, overall, the foundations and development opportunities of the national economy. This happens, for example, when secrecy, organizational barriers and other factors complicate the transfer of technology. However, it may also be due to a structural incompatibility between military and civilian economies (Kubbig 1986, pp. 213-14; Christensen 1989, p. 25).

The inherent complexity of both the military organizations and technologies has been largely neglected in the spin-off debate. Today, the production of arms "is the work of a complex, hierarchical, centralized, and specialization-oriented network which links together governments, military establishments, industries and universities into a highly interpenetrated and mutually reinforcing whole" (Dolman 1981, p. 295). Similarly, modern technologies and their support systems are demanding. Instead of being mere pieces of equipment, modern military systems are families of weapons which combine several major components and have a variety of uses. This complexity means that the spin-off processes cannot be analyzed, as a rule, as simple transfers of knowledge or artefacts from one part of the national economy to the other.

In this context, any meaningful discussion on the relationship between technology and development presupposes that various types of spin-offs are distinguished from each other. They may be categorized both by quantitative and qualitative criteria (Trebilcock 1969, p. 475). In the former case the focus is on the extent to which products and techniques are transferred from the military to the civilian applications. More important, however, are the qualitative spin-offs; new materials, new production processes and new management policies, invented in the military sphere and transplanted in the commercial market.

The qualitative spin-offs may be viewed in the context of the distinction between established and emerging technologies. Established technologies have a safe position in the market or in the bureaucracy, while the emerging technologies are only seeking for the market demand or political and administrative constituencies. Advanced technologies, irrespective of their purpose, are always scarce and expensive to develop. That is why the spin-offs are more significant if the development of military industry, instead of transferring routinized technical solutions, provides impetus to the growth of emerging advanced technologies. In other words, the past, dominant and emerging technologies are not separate from each other, but their relationship also involves complementarities and compatibilities. "New technologies do not necessarily displace older ones: they form a relationship with them, dividing and allocating production" (Cox 1987, p. 318).

Both in the market and in the state system there is a premium on the possession of modern technologies which can be used to strengthen one's position in the competition with rivals. The possession of established advanced technologies is a resource and the access to emerging technologies gives a promise that the power position can be retained or, in the case of ascending nations, strengthened in the future. By investing in emerging technologies, states and companies can make a claim on the future and in that way enhance their power prospects. In reality, the high costs of developing technology create the situation in which only leading transnational companies or national states have sufficient resources to promote R&D across the board.

Military technology is developed primarily for political and military and not for economic reasons. Such reasons include the perception of external threat, search for political prestige and the desire to increase the autonomy of national decision-making (Wulf 1984, pp. 114-15). The primacy of the military purpose is enhanced by the argument that arms production is not an effective means to expand economic potential because of the trade-off effects in economic development. Arms production may even lead to the reduction of economic autonomy as the operation of military industry creates external technological and financial dependencies. In that way the degree of autonomy in the national political decision-making may be curtailed rather than increased.

Indeed, many empirical studies suggest that arms production is inefficient and expensive. It may fuel economic growth in the short run, but it distorts the structure of the national economy in the long run and has only a limited export potential, particularly at present when the demand for weapons is declining and the arms market is saturated. The employment and other positive economic effects of arms production are usually quite limited and may incur considerable opportunity costs. The specific empirical relations depend, however, on the structure of the economy in question and its position in the world market (for example, Ayres 1983; Chan 1988; UN 1988).

On the other hand, there is the historical Sombartian view that the military and warfare have been important agents of technological and organizational change. The allocation of resources for the military has given rise to new industries and has permitted the stablization of their position in the market (Cypher 1987). Furthermore, this perspective points out that in the sixteenth and seventeenth centuries the modern war gave rise to large-scale industrial capitalism (Sombart 1913, pp. 4-6). A more modest argument is that war fosters both technical innovation and longer production series and in that way shapes the capitalist economy (Varga 1982).

The thesis that war and armaments improve industrial efficiency and lead to reforms can, however, be questioned. Rather it may be argued that long periods of peace are more conducive to technological and industrial innovation than warfare. The physical destruction and economic losses engendered by war are always greater than its contribution through increased public spending to economic and technological development. In this view, "warfare is less a cause for industrialism than its shadow and its nemesis" (Nef 1978, pp. 375-8). This is particularly true outside Europe where it is difficult to establish any meaningful positive relationship between warfare and industrial development. Even for Europe, there is surprisingly little historical evidence that "military activity created positive externalities for civilian production given their apparent opportunities" (Mokyr 1990, pp. 183-6).

The planning for war cannot be disentangled from the military innovation. Rosen has suggested that, in order for it to spread, the ideological underpinnings of the technological innovation must contain a theory of victory which must be translated into concrete new tasks. The new theory of victory more than the nature of innovation itself is decisive in the assessment of its value. If the new theory is able to create new career opportunities and other benefits, the underlying innovation has a good chance to become accepted (Rosen 1988, pp. 141-3). The innovation must also be forward-looking and focus on military tasks that will exist some twenty years ahead. This is roughly the time the young officer generation needs to benefit from the new career opportunities (Rosen 1988, p. 167).

The Sombartian view is predicated on the primacy of the state in steering the preparations for war, including the development of military technology. The use of public resources, accumulated by the state, to sponsor technological and organizational innovation gives the military producers time to entrench and protects them from the vagaries of the market. Neither the market nor the military alone could hardly have created an extensive and functioning arms industry. The initiative and protective role of the state, justified by various doctrines of national security and power, has been decisive in underpinning arms development and production.

International Structure and Technology

The international system is cast in a hierarchically structured centre-periphery pattern. The system has two main aspects, the world economy and the international state system. The world economy is driven by the law of value operating in the market and, in concrete terms, by transnational corporations locating their production on the basis of its long-term profitability. The state system is, in turn, driven by the twin policies of expansion and containment on the one hand and by domination and emancipation on the other. The relationship between the world economy and the international state system is complex. They are two distinct spheres of action which interact with, but which cannot be reduced to each other. In a sense, there is a dialectic relationship between the world economy and the international state system as they both condition and shape each other, while retaining their relative autonomy.

In order to improve their relative positions in international political and military rivalries, states make efforts to control economic resources created by production and market exchange. The corporate world tends to resist the policies of states to extend their control to the marketplace, but may call for their support in competition with foreign companies.

On the other hand, states establish barriers to the penetration of transnational corporations into the national economies, in particular in politically and militarily critical sectors. Thus, there are frictions in the relationship between the state and the market: "the tension between these fundamentally different ways of ordering human relationship has profoundly shaped the course of modern history and constitutes the crucial problem in the study of political economy" (Gilpin 1987, pp. 10-11). More specifically, Gill and Law have observed that the dialectic between state and market "involves both domestic and international dimensions of state activity, which seek to reconcile the potentially global reach of economic activity with the socially and territorially specific aspects of political rule" (Gill and Law 1989, p. 479).

Industrialization and underlying technological development is a central process both in the world economy and in interstate relations. In the political theory of what Jones (1988) calls "economic realism", industrialization is usually interpreted as a response of governments to the pressures of international strategic competition. In the neo-mercantilistic world, national capabilities in most important strategic industries are considered an important precondition for national security. Economic resources become inseparable not only from national welfare, but also from external security.

In economic realism, industrialization offers a material basis and instruments for the conduct of external relations. In so doing, industrialization increases the number of political options and provides new techniques to pursue them. "For the manufacturing states, industry thus presented a new means of exercising power and one which was particularly advantageous for as long as there were no technical substitutes or only a finite number of producers" (Pearton 1982, p. 21). In effect, the products of industrialization have been regarded as *the* power resource in states' economic and military competition with other states.

In the world economy, industrialization is a part and parcel of the global economic expansion and accumulation. It is by its very nature an uneven process and gives rise to the emergence of centres and peripheries. Industrialization is thus both a contextual process and a national strategy to promote specific political objectives. It is a reflection of the general tendency of states to enhance their power by the accumulation and enclosure of economic resources. Those resources underpin political projects by which economic and strategic control is expanded in order to improve the relative national gain (Gilpin 1987, pp. 31-4). Economic wealth is an avenue to political power and hence regarded as valuable by the realists.

The international system is hierarchically organized in three layers; centre, semi-periphery and periphery. There is a constant vertical mobility between these layers; historically, a selected group of states rise and decline from one zone of economic activity and political power to another. The centre-periphery structure has both a quantitative and qualitative dimension reflected in the size of states and the nature of their economic processes. Size is, in its essence, a relative phenomenon and may be measured by the share of national resources of the global production or trade.

The nature of economic processes is approximated by the relative labour productivity which tends to be high in the centre and low in the periphery. By combining size and productivity of the national economy it is possible to develop a typology in which the states are classified by their position on the dimensions of relative economic size and labour productivity. David A. Lake (1988, pp. 29-44) has distinguished six categories of states by combining their relative size (large, middle or small) and their relative labour productivity (high or low). According to Lake, the nation's combination of relative size and productivity strongly influences its role in international economic co-operation.

In their vertical mobility the states may move on both dimensions, namely, size and productivity. Increased productivity means that resources are utilized more effectively; as a consequence, the state is able to accumulate economic resources and improve its relative position in the world economy. High power status is more valued than the low one. That is why the states develop strategic economic projects by which they can increase their national power and influence. Such a state policy mobilizes national resources by both direct and indirect measures, and extracts them for political and military efforts (Mastanduno, Lake and Ikenberry 1989, pp. 462-3).

Domestic arms production is one of the strategic projects by which governments promote their ambitions as defined by political realists. Modern arms production requires advanced technologies and materials inputs from several industries. By a complex production process these inputs can be converted into weapons systems and other military products. More specifically, arms production requires a well-developed capital-goods industry supplying machinery and tools to the rest of the industry. Capital-goods production is in the core of the innovation process of the industrial system. It forms the nodal point which links organized science and technology to production. The strategic projects of developing countries are not feasible without the existence of a sufficient capital-goods sector.

The technologically demanding nature of arms production ensures that internationally the industry itself is hierarchically organized and both reflects and reproduces the centre-periphery structure of the world system (Neumann 1984). This creates a constant tension between the political motivation to manufacture arms and the difficulty in establishing an indigenous economic and technological basis for it. The primacy of political motivations makes this tension permanent. In addition to the power motivation, conflicts with other powers and embargoes imposed by the arms suppliers are closely associated with the decision to start developing and producing weapons at home (Peleg 1980).

The peripheral countries seldom have indigenous production of major weapons, but they rely on importation of arms or licence production. Semi-peripheral countries are balancing between the dependencies inherent in the domestic arms production and the search for self-sufficiency justified by the security considerations. Only the centre countries have a sufficient industrial potential to strive for the autonomous production of arms, and even they face difficulties in trying to avoid dependencies on the external world (Wulf 1984; Tuomi and Väyrynen 1982).

The technological element is pertinent in conceptualizing the international centre-periphery structure. In fact, its importance has considerably increased over time. Both scientific research and its technological applications require extensive economic, organizational and human resources. For this reason, differences in the quantity and quality of overall national capabilities have a direct bearing on the ability of individual states to develop an advanced technology base and to utilize it for political purposes.

Technology gaps are real and pervasive in the present world system. They exist not only between developed and developing countries, but also within these groups of countries and between large and small economic and political units. Technology gaps are qualitative in the first place; the more advanced and scarce the technology or skill, the greater the gap between haves and have-nots. Obviously, the qualitative technology gaps correlate strongly with the productivity gaps between national economies.

The qualitative gaps in technology have, in turn, direct connections with the nature of the global arms race. Semi-peripheral and peripheral countries are necessarily one or more steps behind in the process of military innovation. If they try to acquire the most modern weapons, the dualism between military modernity and economic underdevelopment increases and becomes, in the end, impossible to cope with. The search for the technological edge in the military rivalry not only forces the leading military powers to compete with each other, but also to innovate in order to retain their edge in relation to the secondary powers.

Technical performance rather than reliability and cost-effectiveness has become the hallmark in the development of weapons systems. The focus on performance stimulates qualitative arms competition as major powers feel compelled to match the military technological advances by the adversary. It also enhances the complexity of weapons systems and makes them more vulnerable to technical failures (Fallows 1981; Schomacker, Wilke and Wulf 1987, pp. 59-63). This process of escalation often manifests itself in an offence-defence competition rather than in a direct duel between offensive capabilities. Offensive weapons intended to penetrate the defences of the adversary are, as a rule, cheaper and technically easier to develop and produce.

Defensive systems are seldom cost-effective at the margin. Militarily, they tend to engender new instabilities by encouraging the development of counter-offensive weapons to penetrate the defences. Military instabilities, in turn, exacerbate political tensions. In several historical arms races leading military powers have become locked in a mutual technological competition to acquire expensive advanced, high-performance weapons.

Developing countries do not have financial resources and technical skills to compete with centre states in the acquisition and absorption of advanced military technologies. Yet a kind of demonstration effect seduces them to look for novel technological solutions in their efforts to strengthen national security and increase political power. In developed countries military industry is usually integrated with the rest of the economy, even though the specific requirements of the military may give rise to unconventional and exotic technological solutions (Schomacker, Wilke and Wulf 1987, pp. 63-6). In developing countries, the military's predilection for advanced technology tends to create more serious tensions between the technological modernity of the military systems and the disadvantaged-factor endowment in the economy.

The impact of arms production and arms purchases differs between large and small countries. In the production and distribution of technology, size is relevant for several reasons; provided that the society is effectively organized it helps to appropriate the benefits of applying new technologies, to exploit the economies of scale and to pass the threshold level of R&D above which it becomes industrially useful (Clark 1985, pp. 119-20). Large size does not necessarily bring success, but it provides potential which can be utilized for this end.

If small countries want to become active in the technology market they have to concentrate their scarce domestic resources to selected areas of innovation and to orient at an early stage to the export market (Walsh 1988). The development of an effective system of production and diffusion of technology calls for concentration, and gives, in small countries, to a few centres of power, instruments to consolidate their authority and to crowd out other varieties of human action (Winner 1986, pp. 47-9). Relatively speaking, the degree of concentration may not be as high in large countries, but in them a similar process of selection creates centres of power that, in absolute terms, have stronger, external consequences.

Size is certainly not the only, and not even the most important, determinant of the development and diffusion of technology. Historically, technology has become more diversified and complex, putting premium on specialization. It helps companies to maintain or expand their market share and otherwise to recover material benefits from the market. Specialization is, however, difficult to convert into control over market. Specialized market power is limited, among other things, by the cross-sectoral linkages which enable big corporations, operating in several sectors, to regulate the activities of small companies.

Organizations, Technology and the Arms Race

More decisive for the exercise of social power than the nature of technology is the character of agents that develop and utilize it. Since it may have a dynamics of its own, these agents may not shape the development of technology itself, so much as its introduction into the military doctrines and institutions. This is consistent with the view that there is a mutual interaction between technology and social forces. "Technology is the means of solving the practical problems of societies, but what problems are to be solved and which kinds of solutions are acceptable are determined by those who hold social power" (Cox 1987, p. 21).

Technology and agents are not independent of each other. On the contrary, mutually compatible patterns of technologies, policies and productive organization, termed by Dosi (1982) as "technological paradigms", tend to emerge. Such paradigms are internally consistent so long as its constituent elements develop in synchrony with each other. The paradigm faces a crisis if technology and organization become incompatible or if policy is at a crossroads with both or either of them.

Military technology is more directly shaped by public policy than by non-military technology, as governments keep it under close supervision as a part of security policy. Thus, a crisis in the technological paradigm can be created by the government whose policy demands significantly deviate from the technological basis or the productive organization of society. In fact, the level and nature of technological development and productive organization considerably constrain the military policy choices.

Constraints faced by individual countries naturally differ, primarily by the level of their economic development. Among developing countries, those with a certain industrial potential are plagued by balance-of-payment problems and dependence on the imported intermediary products for arms manufacturing. The underdeveloped countries struggle, in turn, with the elemental dilemma of how scarce resources should be allocated between various imperative needs. (Nzongola-Ntalaja and Bigman 1989, pp. 249-61). In the former case, the economic effects of military industrialization should be scrutinized at the margins, while in the latter case the choices are more absolute.

In general, an ambitious military policy calls for a bottom-up approach. In order to avoid a crisis in the technological paradigm, the government aims to strengthen the nation's overall technological basis and to restructure its productive organization. In that way the country is expected to embark upon a long-term strategy which purports to permit an effective development and production of military weapons and to help in avoiding incompatibilities between technology, policy and organization. The strategy of establishing an industrial base compatible with the interests of ambitious arms procurement programmes has been followed, among others, by South Korea and, to a lesser degree, Taiwan (Nolan 1986, pp. 105-8).

Mary Kaldor has discovered a technological paradigm in her studies on the historical development of military technology. In her paradigm the major weapons systems and their prime contractors tend to continue and to maintain the stability and permanence of the military-industrial structure. Instead of changing the structure, the technological dynamics is geared to improve the performance of weapons; their speed, versatility and destructiveness. The development and production of military technology in a stagnant institutional environment fosters "baroque technology" in which an improvement in military effectiveness requires an increasing amount of resources. Major weapons systems become institutional forces in their own right. They tend to define the lines of command within the armed forces and the military-industrial structure of the economy. At the same time they become less functional in military terms (Kaldor 1981, pp. 11-28; see also Fallows 1981).

Kaldor's observations hint to the importance of organizational factors in the arms race. Technology retains its significance, but in a constrained manner: "the direction of technical change, it can be argued, is confined within limits that are defined by the persistence of military and industrial institutions" (Kaldor 1981, p. 18). This analysis expands the empirical work by Jacques Gansler showing how the unit costs and the performance of weapons systems tend to increase in tandem. The strong concentration of military R&D and the permanence of the military-industrial structure form barriers of entry to the market and do not encourage new, invention-oriented companies. Military R&D contracts with big companies become a kind of subsidy which supports performance-oriented technology programmes having a potential to fill the production lines (Gansler 1980, pp. 99-105).

Most theories of military innovation stress the intrinsic conservatism of military institutions rejecting new technologies that would potentially upset the established balance of forces within the military organization. The new weapons system may be rejected altogether or, if that is not feasible, it is not efficiently incorporated into the structure and tactics of the armed forces. Only the war reveals the gap between the doctrine and practice which the military conservatism has brought about. The resistance faced by the plans to introduce the machine gun to the US Army provides illuminating material in this regard (Armstrong 1982; see also Pearton 1982, pp. 31-2).

The preservation of a nation's international status presupposes that the military-industrial system must constantly receive new technological inputs. They can be gained only from the basic science community. If the technology outruns basic science, a technology barrier emerges (Bradbury 1981, p. 283). Such a barrier is not necessarily a problem within the military system. On the contrary, it would alleviate the pressures of organizational and doctrinal change and satisfy the conservative trait in the military thinking.

The technology barrier can be a problem, however, in the military-industrial competition with the adversaries, and raise the possibility of losing the rivalry. In order to avoid the loss, the military becomes interested not only in sponsoring and controlling the military R&D, but also the basic civilian research. "The military's growing interest in controlling the results of research is directly linked to the increasing importance these results play in the development of military technologies" (Dickson 1988, p. 111; see also Thee 1986, pp. 103-110).

The elimination of potential instabilities in the technological paradigm calls for a policy in which the military is able to control the results of military-related science and to integrate technology in the military organizations. Such an arrangement "tames" the technology and makes its effects predictable within the organization. The organizational entrenchment of technology, not the autonomy of science, lends it autodynamic features and undermines the possibilities of political control. This suggests that techno-structures and other forces associated with technology are gaining in importance, condition political choices, and make disarmament more difficult. The alternative view posits that technology is primarily an instrument of politics; it can be used purposively by the actors to advance their own interests and goals, both good and bad (Gilpin 1972).

Technology and Economic Dynamics

The acquisition of military technology, whether by domestic procurement or purchases from abroad, cannot be separated from politics. It is usually based on the mixture of voluntary and involuntary motives. The voluntary aspect is manifested in the long-term strategy to increase the national military capability in order to gain more political and territorial power. The involuntary aspect of acquisition policies derives from the need to produce or purchase weapons to repel an imminent external threat. In everyday politics the voluntary and involuntary motives are usually entangled in a rather inseparable whole.

The contents and methods of the voluntary acquisition strategy are shaped according to the available economic resources, while the involuntary policy imposes a kind of economic emergency on the country. During the upswing of a long economic cycle, such as the Kondratieff wave, economic resources are augmented and the opportunities of national economic and military expansion increase. During the downswing the overall scarcity in society limits the acquisition of military weapons. Of course, the availability of economic resources alone does not determine the acquisition policy; it rather sets limits within which the decisions have to be made.

There is a general view, associated with Joseph A. Schumpeter in the first place, that technological innovations correlate with the long-term dynamics of national economies. Briefly, the Schumpeterian argument goes as follows. Various elements of technological innovations take a relatively long time to mature, but at a certain point, usually the transition period from the slow to a more rapid economic growth, the new innovations cluster into a sustained technological advance. The change in the capitalist system comes from inside when entrepreneurs carry out new combinations of the factors of production and set up a new production function which transforms the economy.

Technological innovations can be product or process innovations which either alter the basic structure of the economy or merely improve the products or processes. The product innovations are central in the long-term economic dynamics. They generate a climate of investment optimism, increase demand and employment and accelerate economic growth. Product innovations are a means of exiting from depression: "an upturn in production tends to dampen innovation, while a downturn in production stimulates innovation". Innovations follow production by five to ten years (Goldstein 1988, p. 224).

The clusters or swarms of innovations, as Schumpeter called them, together with appropriate infrastructural investments, create new leading industrial sectors. They dominate the span of a long cycle from depression through boom to stagnation. Stagnation starts when the new technologies are fully integrated in the economy and their productive and demand potential decreases. The companies focus on process and improvement innovations rather than on basic product innovations in order to cut back their costs. The main goal is to survive in the market which is expanding only slowly or even contracting (Freeman 1983; van Duijn 1983).

The leading industrial sectors, emerging in the boom phase of the Kondratieff wave, shape both the civilian and military systems of production. The leading sector complexes are unfolded in a sequence generated by a mixture of consumer demands and the requirements of industry and of transport. These complexes have comprised manufactured textiles, the steam engine, iron technology and the railways, steel, electricity, chemical industry and automobile (Rostow 1975, p. 751). The complexes are not defined primarily by their absolute size, but by their impact on economic growth. It is greatest in the early phases of the sector's development when it integrates technological, financial and human resources into a bundle, and experiences diminishing returns after the process of maturing has been completed (Thompson 1990, pp. 211-12).

Obviously, long economic cycles, technological innovations and industrial restructuring change the political power structures of societies. Social groups associated with the rising leading sectors not only reap more economic benefits, but also tend to demand and gain more socio-political power, penetrating into political institutions. In the power game, the new groups use the slogans of modernity to defeat the traditionalists of the previous long cycle.

The technological history can be placed in the context of the long-term economic dynamics. However, it has to be kept in mind that their relationship is very complex and it is influenced by a host of third factors. The leading industrial sector is the central link between the nature of productive technology and the long-term movements of capitalist economies (Rostow 1978).

The first Kondratieff wave from 1787 to 1842 was linked with the emergence of new technologies and sectors - textiles, coal and iron - which paved the way for the first industrial revolution. The second wave from 1843 to 1897 was generated by the railway boom: especially the upswing of 1850-72 witnessed the expansion of the railway complex, and various technological and organizational innovations associated with it. The expansion of railways was concentrated mainly in Europe and North America, but trunk lines were also built in India and Latin America. In addition to their civilian economic potential, railways had profound military significance and, in effect, they became a decisive factor in modern war and the mobilization for it (Pearton 1982, pp. 69-76).

Another technological revolution took place in shipping; in the middle of the nineteenth century steam and steel replaced sails and wood in the ships of the line. Both of these changes in the transportation technology required steel and coal and in that way advances in heavy engineering and mining. They also changed the geopolitical equation as the new coal-burning ships needed coaling stations and local bases more urgently than the sailing ships (Pearton 1982, pp. 54-5). As a matter of fact, both "steamships and railways . . . were powerful machines of iron and steam, swift and punctual means of travel, the most visible of the innovations transforming the world" (Headrick 1988, p. 49).

During the third Kondratieff wave from 1898 to 1947, and in particular during the economic upswing from 1898 to 1914, the importance of the railway and shipping complexes persisted. Steel industry and engineering became more efficient and sophisticated, and the chemical and electrical industries started their gradual rise. The electrical revolution was apparently a chief characteristic of the third wave; it created a wide range of innovations and new industries, and produced and disseminated power more economically and effectively than ever before. Electrical industries were associated with the emergence of information technologies which bridged the world by cables and radio waves (Hall and Preston 1988).

The development of the automobile and the airplane as means of transportation started with basic innovations at the turn of the century. However, they matured as leading sectors only during the interwar period, which is often considered a depression period. This is not necessarily an anomaly in my argument since the economic performance in the 1920s was in most countries rather solid and continued the upswing of the prewar period before the breakdown in the early 1930s.

The automobile and aeroplane complexes carried over to the post-World War II period in a manner somewhat similar to that in which the railway complex had done earlier. The industrial structure was based on the mass production of standardized investment goods, including vehicles and consumer durables. The most sophisticated technological innovations of the postwar era came from nuclear power and the microchip. Nuclear power was augmented to produce cheap energy and remove the uncertainties of supply. The microchip symbolized the arrival of an information society based on the huge increase in the processing power and memory of computers that permitted the utilization of vast amounts of data. In a word, the postwar era has been dominated by the development and spread of information technology whose power has expanded in an almost unbelievable manner since the beginning of the twentieth century.

This historical review shows that economic dynamics and technological development have interacted closely with each other, although the critical factor of causality is difficult to establish between them (Rosenberg and Frischtak 1984, pp. 8-11). Each successive cluster of technological innovations, associated with economic fluctuations, has transformed the technological preconditions of warfare and military operations. Technological innovations have not, however, directly determined the nature and functions of weaponry (Väyrynen 1983; Väyrynen 1990). On the other hand, some long-wave theorists have argued for the reversed direction of causality: wars spark economic cycles and innovations (Goldstein 1988, pp. 32-9).

Independently of the causal direction, new technologies have increased the effectiveness, flexibility and the range of military operations and have thus opened new dimensions in the character and effects of warfare. As a consequence, the substance of war has changed from limited, slow-moving operations to more rapid and total encounters of potentially global scale. The time available to policy-makers to perceive and to react has been shortened significantly, and they have been subjected increasingly to contextual influences which are outside their direct control. In the explanation of war, the volitional approach, stressing the role of governmental decision-making, has given way to an environmental perspective (Domke 1988).

Each upswing of the long economic cycle has given rise to new concepts of military technology and warfare and to a new sector of military production (Kaldor 1987, pp. 148-52). The railway complex facilitated large-scale troop movements, used for the first time in the Austro-Prussian War of 1866 and in the Franco-Prussian war of 1870-71. The troop movements were co-ordinated by telegraph. The ability to mobilize armies and concentrate them on the front became the yardstick of their military performance. The impact of technology on warfare carried over to the next long cycle and influenced, through the war plans, the conduct of the early phases of World War I. Thus, the first Kondratieff wave and its leading sectors gave rise to a total war, and "turned the war itself into a question of managing complex systems" (van Creveld 1989, pp. 158-61).

In technological development the navy has, as a rule, been more innovative than the army. In Britain, this was obviously due to the navy's liberal tradition and its general political approval. Also, in France and Germany the navy was liberally oriented, but in addition investment in technology was considered a way of overcoming British superiority (Pearton 1982, p. 53). The effects of the second cluster of technological innovations were, indeed, more immediately felt in the navy than in the army. In the navy there was a constant struggle between safety and manoeuvrability on the one hand and the firepower and armour on the other. The battleships became bigger and more expensive and, as a consequence, more vulnerable and less usable (Garden 1989, pp. 8-9).

Both in the navy and army, new means of electrical communication altered the nature of warfare. On land, telegraph and telephone helped to control and co-ordinate troop movements, while on sea new command technologies made the naval attacks more mobile and accurate and hence more destructive. Technology genuinely altered the nature of naval strategy (McNeill 1982, pp. 277-85). Before World War I, advances in the chemical industry were applied to develop, stockpile and, ultimately, to use nerve gases. In a way, World War I was the chemists' war, as witnessed at Verdun and the Somme.

In World War II and thereafter, bombers, missiles and aircraft carriers became the symbols of technological primacy and prowess. They combined in a complex manner new materials, jet engines and electronics. With the development of the atomic bomb, their munitions were based on fissile materials. Both in size and quality, these weapons platforms and systems were unprecedented. Gradually, the increasing use of electronics in military hardware has made it possible to reduce its size and make its uses more flexible and accurate. In general, the electronic revolution has interlinked the modern military technology with operations in the battlefield.

The sheer size and vulnerability of aircraft carriers and strategic missile systems has created large battle units which have a hierarchical organization and strong concentration of military power. On the other hand, the emergence of the precision-guided munitions (PGMs) and effective means of communication on the battlefield now permits the decentralization of units. The technological and organizational changes permitting decentralization facilitate, in turn, the emergence of new military doctrines, such as the non-offensive defence, that favour non-nuclear forces.

The growing importance of advanced electronics and robotics in warfare suggests that the control of these technologies will confer considerable military benefits in the future. In the words of one observer "the true strength of the forces in the future will be increasingly manifested by sophisticated technology for command, communications, intelligence, and reconnaissance and for the launching and guidance of robotic, air, ground and sea weapons in a broad variety of forms" (Ramo 1988, p. 17). At present, technology is critically important in the military sphere. It is not necessarily in command, however, as it can be significantly limited and augmented by political decisions and organizational arrangements.

For sheer structural reasons, the development of advanced technology cannot be initiated any more from military R&D and production systems. Especially, the British and US overall economic potential has, relatively speaking, declined in comparison to upwardly mobile countries. This has meant that as the share absorbed by the military of the total national economic resources has not generally increased, the funding of the military industrial base has, again in relative terms, decreased. Increasing or stagnant relative military burdens are not necessarily results of the drive for militarization, but consequences of slow growth. Downward mobility places more resource constraints on the public policy-making and undermines the efforts to sustain an extensive and autonomous military sector. To alleviate the dilemma, the state must try to strengthen the nation's overall economic and technological base and commercialize at least some aspects of the military procurement (Perry 1989, pp. 89-91).

In concrete terms, this means that in declining states a strong spin-off effect from military to civilian innovations can hardly operate in practice. Instead, pressures increase to build on the spin-on processes derived from the active promotion of the civilian technological base. In this context it has been observed, in reference to the United States, that "the direction of influence may even have been reversed: military technologies now appear to depend on advances in civilian applications" (Cyert and Mowery 1989, p. 34; see also Christensen 1989, pp. 29-30).

In other words, in declining powers the funding of basic civilian research is more conducive to the development of military technology than the large-scale allocation of funds to military R&D. To maintain its edge in military technology, the state has first to regain its economic standing. This calls for the need to "separate the goals and benefits of government support for technology from defense spending and to consider a broader conception of national economic interests" (Kuttner 1991, p. 197). Naturally, the technical details of weapons have to be developed by the arms manufacturers and their specialists.

The relationship between economic development and military potential is even more vexing in large but relatively less-developed countries which face the choice between the civilian and economic allocation of resources. The Soviet Union and China, which both have been centrally planned, provide obvious examples of such countries. The first lesson of their experiences is that even though the military industry is not safe from supply disruptions and does not even always have the priority among industrial sectors, it tends to squeeze out the most valuable and scarce inputs from the "shortage economy" (Davis 1990). The other lesson is that in a stagnant economy of a great power a debate emerges between economic pragmatists and military conservatives on the existing and desirable relationship between economic development and military allocation.

Elements of such a debate can be discerned both in the United States and Britain, but it has been much more active in the Soviet Union and China. In the first half of the 1980s, Chinese pragmatists and conservatives differed on the proper level of military spending in relation to the goals of the economic development strategy. These two groups agreed that over a long term a healthy economy is a precondition for a viable military defence, but they disagreed on the present contribution of the military to economic development and on the depth of necessary cutbacks in troop strengths. Pragmatists favoured deep reductions, while the conservatives preferred to implement only a token reorganization of forces. The gist of the argument, which ended in a tenuous compromise, was that:

> pragmatists saw a major cutback of the military strengthening national security in the long term by expanding and improving the country's economic base, which in turn could then support additional military spending and maintain a more sophisticated military posture. The conservatives saw the implications of reduction in more pessimistic and immediate terms, specifically that the PLA's strength rests principally on its size and that this is one of the basic premises of the country's military doctrine. (Cheung 1988, p. 764)

Recently, the case of Japan has been explored from the opposite vantage point. It has been suggested that its strong base in civilian and dual-use technologies, such as semiconductors and new materials, would permit a major expansion of arms production in the future. "Japan now holds the lead in extremely wide-range of these dual-use technologies, and is moving rapidly toward domination in others". Its transition to military power is constrained only by political considerations, not by the lack of technological basis (Dower 1989, pp. 21-2). The rise of the spin-on effect underlines the relevance of technological and organizational linkages and isomorphisms between the military and the civilian production systems.

The reverse question is, then, whether the spin-off process can operate succesfully in upwardly mobile countries, which have, relatively speaking, more economic resources at their disposal, or whether their militarization also derives its strength from the strengthening of its civilian economic and technolological base. My tentative answer is that even in their case the spin-on process is in general more significant, that is, the economic growth has not been initiated primarily by the military motives and arrangements. The effects of the spin-off process are, however, visible and depend on the specific international context of the upwardly mobile country and on the specific institutional arrangements between the military industry, the state and the civilian economy.

Security, Power and Development

The chief aim of this study is to explore the relationships between the civilian and military technologies and their connections on the one hand and the nature and pace of economic development on the other. These relationships are both historically and spatially variable and obviously also depend on such factors as the structure and the level of development of the national economy. A. F. Mullins, Jr., has specified four potential relationships, considering both the spin-off and spin-on processes, between development and military capability. He considers especially the problem of whether development and military capability are or are not necessary for each other's growth (Mullins 1987, pp. 12-14).

It is to be expected that the expansion of economic resources is needed to augment military capabilities and that the opposite can be true only in times of internal or external crises. This consensus is echoed by Paul Kennedy who concludes that "once their productive capacity was enhanced, countries would normally find it easier to sustain the burdens of paying for large-scale armaments in peacetime and of maintaining and supplying large armies and fleets in wartime". Kennedy expands this point by adding that "if, however, too large a proportion of the state's resources is diverted from wealth creation and allocated instead to military purposes, then that is likely to lead to a weakening of national power over the long term" (Kennedy 1987, p. xvi). In addition to military overspending at home, the strategic overextension abroad may also contribute to a similar process of erosion in the nation's economic standing.

Both the United States and Russia are now facing the dilemma that long-term relative decline in economic growth and productivity erodes their strategic strength (although the Russian economic crisis is certainly deeper than that of the United States). This affects both their domestic conditions and their mutual relations and alignment with third countries, including the regional power centres in the Third World. That is why "future superpower national security policy will be increasingly determined by the growing influence of economic performance on strategic competitiveness and by recognition of the critical role of this relationship" (Cohen and Wilson 1988, p. 102).

Given the virtual consensus on the existence of the spin-on effect, the question remains, however, whether military capabilities are required for economic development or whether these factors are not related at all or correlate negatively. The potential positive impact of military capabilities on economic development can be interpreted both in political and economic terms. The economic argument relies on the spin-off effect, while the political argument states that only a nation secured by deterrence and defence can safely develop its economic potential. In this view the abolition of military insecurity does absorb economic resources, but its neglect may lead to conquest by a hostile power, which is even more costly than the maintenance of a sufficient national army.

In an empirical analysis a distinction should be made between military security and military capabilities. Unit-level military capabilities cannot be directly translated into security, which is more of a contextual factor. For practical reasons, the military dimension must be operationalized primarily by the capability factors and its various components such as military spending, armament programmes and troop levels.

A realistic conclusion of this conceptual exploration could be that military security as a contextual phenomenon is a necessary, but obviously not a sufficient, precondition for economic development. Military capabilities are, in turn, neither a necessary nor a sufficient precondition for economic growth. Mullins (1987, pp. 12-13) has captured the relationships well: "development permits the creation of military capability, it does not require it, that military capability allows development but does not ensure it". The multidimensional nature of military and economic issues and the existence of a host of third factors makes it difficult to establish any unequivocal relationships between these dimensions. Finally, one should not exaggerate the role of military spending as a source of economic ills, but should compare it in a prudent manner with their other causes (Ball 1988, p. 392).

Statistical analyses help to define exact relationships between military capabilities and economic changes in specific temporal or spatial contexts. I am sceptical, however, of their ability to capture significant historical relationships between military allocations and socio-economic development. Statistical analyses may be able to define, for example, short-term economic effects of military expenditures, but they are hardly able to tackle long-term structural consequences of military spending and weapons acquisitions. In addition, statistical exercises may have value in studying individual countries, but their results are either difficult to generalize to the systemic level or to place in a systemic context. Yet the systemic level affects both military allocations and economic development and hence shapes their bivariate relationship.

In the study of complex issues and relations it is prudent to believe in comparative case studies in which a relatively small number of units is intensively studied and compared. In comparison to simple case studies, such a comparative research design is considered superior for the purposes of theory development. I also happen to believe more in dynamic than in static analyses of social relations; the process itself is often a significant explanatory factor. Socio-economic relations are usually asymmetrically organized. That is why the centre-periphery model of international relations is an appropriate starting point for the present type of research. Contrary to a common misconception, the centre-periphery model is dynamic by its character as it postulates a constant upward and downward mobility of the actors. The structure remains, but the relative positions of actors are changing over time. This conclusion does not depend upon the theoretical approach chosen. Political realism, the world-system analysis and, with some caveats, the liberal approach can agree on this proposition. The premises for its acceptance are different, however. Political realism focuses on the national distribution of capabilities and its changes, the world-system analysis is primarily interested in the system dynamics of the core, semi-periphery and periphery, while the liberal school explores the role of states in relation to individuals and markets.

This study singles out four countries in roughly two different time periods for intensive empirical analysis. They all are or have been major powers, either globally or in their own regional context. Japan before World War I and Brazil after World War II can be characterized as rising powers. During these periods they have left their peripheral status and developed into semi-peripheral countries. Their ultimate aim has been to join the core of the world economy; Japan has in a miraculous way accomplished this task.

Arms production has been for both Japan and Brazil a political strategy to consolidate their position in the international hierarchy and to enhance their politico-military autonomy *vis-à-vis* the pressures emanating from the global centres of economic power. In semi-peripheral countries military production is politically motivated; independence in military production and in its industrial basis is a goal in itself as they strengthen national political sovereignty. The political motivation behind the indigenous arms industry means that its economic effects are regarded by the policy-makers as secondary: "the achievement of self-sufficiency in defense . . . is an imperative that will not yield to calculations of relative inefficiencies and diseconomies, nor can the defense-industrialization path pursued by third world governments be expected to follow strictly the curves of comparative advantage" (Nolan 1986, p. 5).

While the political primacy accorded to the domestic arms industry reveals the genuine political preferences of the decision-makers, there are also real domestic and international constraints on the mobilization of national resources for military uses. Michael Barnett has developed a framework in which various resource mobilization strategies can be analyzed. He suggests that states start by an accommodation strategy in which the existing policy instruments are utilized in order to accommodate the societal condition to the imperatives of resource extraction. This strategy often proves to be too timid, however, and either the restructural strategy or international strategy is adopted. The restructural strategy either centralizes the policy-making by increasing the direct control of the state over resources or liberalizes parts of the economy to increase productivity and innovation. The international approach favours economic and military alignments with foreign powers in order to redistribute the costs of military preparations. These three strategic choices are closely conditioned by domestic factors such as the need to maintain political stability and to keep those practising military ambition in political power (Barnett 1990, pp. 542-6).

The idea of technological and industrial trajectories is based on the simple notion that the military technology and arms industry change over time. The concept of technological paradigm suggests, in turn, that in the course of this change the relationship of technology to policies and productive organization is transformed. In that way the relative economic costs and benefits and their distribution are altered, and have an impact on the political decisions pertaining to the arms industry. Edward Kolodziej has stressed how the initial strategic-political incentives of arms production are gradually modified as the economic constraints are understood by policy makers. Then, the pressure to export increases, the optimal utilization of resources is emphasized and international co-operation to share the R&D expenses is expanded. Gradually, these "subsidiary economic-technological considerations assume an independent character and claim on national priorities" (Kolodziej 1987, pp. 305-7).

In that way the arms industry is gradually integrated into the technological strategy and economic structure of the country, and the industry's implications for security policy are placed in a broader societal and economic context. Over time, economic consequences become more important and it is pertinent to query and evaluate their nature and magnitude. The basic argument here is that in upwardly mobile countries, especially if they are climbing from semi-periphery to the core, the development of military technology and military industry may support the expansion and diversification of the civilian economy. This hypothesis is in line with Miles Kahler's view that in mature dominant powers the opportunity costs of military spending tend to be higher and the fiscal effects negative. In upwardly mobile countries which have not yet achieved dominance, the structural economic constraints on military production are tighter and the cost-benefit calculation more careful. This helps to explain why the linkage between military ambition and economic development, mediated by the policy style, may be positive in semi-peripheral countries (Kahler 1988, pp. 447-8).

In particular in the context of international economic and power dynamics, the spin-off argument is theoretically and empirically more interesting than the opposite spin-on argument which posits that the progress in civilian industries underpins the qualitative development of military technology. The spin-on argument is, after all, rather self-evident, while the spin-off process can operate in several different ways. The most typical linkage between military and civilian technologies is the direct impact of the military research and development; military research gives rise to materials and products that can be utilized also for civilian purposes. It is commonly argued that the military road to economic development is not particularly cost-effective; the allocation of similar amounts of resources to civilian projects would have produced at least equal results. The Israeli case provides evidence that extensive military production does not solve the dilemmas of the national economy. About 40 per cent of Israel's 20 leading industrial companies are highly dependent on military production. Despite the fact that these companies often operate at the advanced end of technology, they have not been able to convert Israel into an export-driven economy (Mintz 1985).

However, in this context it is useful to remember the observation that: "even if it is true that those advances in civilian technology that spin off from military R&D could have been achieved faster and cheaper by a massive civilian R&D effort, such a civilian effort would never have been undertaken" (Dumas 1988, p. 295). This being the case, the allocation of resources on political and security grounds to military R&D obviously influences the direction of technical progress, as the development of computers and micro-electronics shows. Yet it is hardly an efficient way to transform a nation's economic resources into productive goods (Reppy 1985).

Another reason for the operation of the spin-off effect is the protection which the military interests provide for advanced technologies. This resembles the infant-industry argument in the debate on economic development strategies. The protection of the domestic technology market for the sake of national security is supposed to give companies time to develop their technologies before they are subjected to foreign competition (Kahler 1988, p. 426). In reality, agriculture and military industry are the most protected fields of economic activity. The foreign takeover of key defence contractors is looked upon by governments with askance and is usually prevented by the intervention of state. Only those co-operative deals blessed by the government can be realized.

On the other hand, there is a wealth of arguments and evidence against the spin-off effects. The most common one is the assertion that military R&D and military spending in general tend to crowd out civilian technological innovation and investment. According to this argument there is a negative allocation effect which deprives the key civilian industries of the resources they would need in order to advance.

Another reason for the negative impact of military capabilities on the civilian economy concerns the inefficiency of military industries. It is engendered by the lack of competition, the nature of the contract system between companies and the government, and the high transaction costs of companies. These inefficiencies are visible in both the national and collaborative transnational weapons projects (Weida and Gertcher 1986, pp. 136-8; Deutsch and Schöpp 1987, p. 339; Hartley 1987). Still another factor put forward to explain the lack of spin-off effects is the overspecification of military products. Military technology is too complex and performance-oriented to be cost-effective in civilian applications (Weida and Gertcher 1986, pp. 139-40).

The Structure of the Study

The nature of linkages between military and civilian industries is necessarily complex. It does not depend only on the economic and political organization of the country or on the state of its technology. The strength and nature of linkages are also accounted for by the country's relative international position and its dynamics. In this collection of comparative case studies I will scrutinize two declining powers, England before World War I and the United States in the 1970s and the 1980s, and two rising powers, Japan from the Meiji Restoration to World War I and Brazil during the last few decades (see Table 1.1).

Table 1.1: The Comparative Basis of the Study

	The rate of economic growth	
	Accelerated	*Decelerated*
Rising Power	Japan 1868-1914	Brazil 1960-1990
Declining Power	Great Britain 1897-1914	The United States 1960-1990

The comparative framework of the study can be further elaborated by considering two different phases of the long economic cycles: the period from 1897 to 1914 was characterized by an accelerated economic growth, while the 1970s and the 1980s experienced a decelerated growth pattern. The framework covers, in other words, four different combinations of long-cycle phases and the direction of vertical mobility. Each of these combinations will be illuminated by an empirical case study.

The basic thesis of this study is that military industrialization does not necessarily have detrimental economic consequences, although it often does. On the contrary, there can be positive spin-offs from military industrialization to civilian economic development provided, among other things, that the country in question is ascending in the hierarchy of states. The link between military and civilian industrialization is probably even stronger if the world economy is expanding during the period under scrutiny. There is very little if any spin-off if the state is declining, one reason for this being that the military consumption undermines civilian development efforts by crowding out scarce resources and technological skills. The negative relationship is even stronger if the growth of world economy is slow or outright negative.

The centre-periphery structure of the international system is not at all unimportant in this context. In the periphery, a main problem is that military industrialization can proceed only if there is a sufficient capacity in capital goods. They have to be purchased from the industrialized countries, and in that way peripheral economies are hooked to the leading industrial powers. Using Bhagavans (1979, pp. 28-9) expression, such a relationship creates the "technological dependency of the primary kind". To overcome this dependency the peripheral countries must be clever and clear, first, about their objectives, and secondly, in devising methods by which they can avoid the trap of excessive technological dependence but yet safeguard their own economic and security interests.

Chapter 2
Military Production and the Rise of Japan

The Meiji Restoration

States and societies seldom change unless they are challenged from outside. In particular, closed and hierarchically organized societies are able to retain their established order if they can keep the world out. In such societies internal impulses, whether they are due to technological dynamism, changing social values or structural transformations, can be contained by the power elite. But when an isolated society, voluntarily or involuntarily, is opened to external influences, the pace of change can be rapid and it is very effectively reorganized. One of the critical questions is whether the transformation is directed from above or the external pressures lead to an uncontrolled, perhaps chaotic change.

The Tokugawa *bakufu* faced a strong Western challenge from 1853 on. Japan was politically disunited, militarily weak and economically underdeveloped. Its vulnerability extended across the board and was heightened by the growing Western interests in the Far East in general and in Japan in particular. The Tokugawa elite perceived the Western powers both as a threat and a model which should be emulated. In fact, these two perceptions were interrelated; the elite thought that by learning from the West, the Japanese indigenous ability to cope with its challenge would be strengthened. The mixture of two policies, i.e. to assimilate foreign influences into domestic society and to resist them, thus had a common foundation; heady nationalism which placed a high premium on the political unification of country.

The acquisition of Western-style weaponry was started in Japan even before the Perry expedition in 1855. In the 1840s the perception spread that the Chinese had been defeated in the Opium War because of the technical supremacy of the Western guns and steamships. Several feudal domains, *han*, started at their own initiative to copy Western technology and produce guns and ships. In addition, the Tokugawa *bakufu* started to manufacture arms and established the Yokosuka and Nagasaki Ironworks, the latter with Dutch assistance. The French contributed significantly to the construction of the Yokosuka Shipyard. The Tokyo Arsenal was established to produce cannons (Fugushima 1966, pp. 189-90 and Mitsukuni 1985, pp. 193-8).

Western military technology was gradually introduced in the 1850s and the reliance on it continued throughout the 1860s (Norman 1940, pp. 118-20). In particular, French and British military expertise was utilized to modernize the military establishment. For this purpose, the Tokugawa government imported from the West not only engineers but entire factories, an early example of turnkey plants. The objective was to unite and centralize the Tokugawa state by military and technical modernization (Lehmann 1982, p. 151; Jansen 1971, pp. 213-14). By purchasing military technology from the West, the *bakufu* aimed to outclass its adversaries, Satsuma *han* and Choshu *han* in south-western Japan.

In response, the opposition forces also started to modernize their military forces by purchasing weapons from the West. The *shogunate* tried to arrest this trend by a blockade on the acquisition of foreign weapons. In 1866 Satsuma and Choshu concluded an alliance to oppose the Tokugawa government. This alliance, supported by the British to counterbalance the French influence on the *shogunate*, inaugurated the final decline of the feudal system. The military weakness of the Tokugawa *bakufu*, which the external support could not significantly remedy, was a main reason for its demise, but this process was also assisted by the growing national awareness of the need to unify and reorganize the country. Otherwise, the society may not have been able to survive in the world of intensifying competition between major powers (Jansen 1971, pp. 220-2; Lehmann 1982, pp. 150-1).

The restoration of power by the Satsuma-Choshu alliance to the emperor Meiji in 1868 was closely associated with the arrangement of Japan's relations with the West. The new leaders had become convinced of the Western military superiority and advocated more strongly than the *shogunate* the development of commerce and the acquisition of Western military techniques (Beasley 1982, p. 97 and 111). Continuity in the Japanese society was still its hallmark, but the need for reform had become overpowering.

There was an interesting parallel development in China and Japan from the 1860s on. The Meiji Restoration can be compared with the Self-strengthening Movement in China which was launched in 1861. This movement aimed to modernize the Chinese society by importing Western technology and institutions. Its basic philosophy was to retain peace by diplomacy and use that respite for strengthening the country by adopting the superior techniques of the barbarians to beat them. Obviously, the Japanese policy of acquiring Western weapons and military technology, stimulated by the Chinese experience, in turn caused concern in China because of the animosities between the two countries.

The Self-strengthening Movement in China had an explicit military component. The development of military industries was emphasized; the Kiangnan arsenal was established in 1865 to manufacture firearms and the Foochow Dockyard was launched in 1866 to produce ships for the coastal defence against the threats from the sea. The military industries were the springboard of China's economic modernization, even though practically all the materials and technology had to be imported. By the middle of the 1870s it was realized, however, that full-scale modernization cannot take place unless the management of industries is reorganized, a market element is added to the reform, and the infrastructures and civilian industries are significantly developed (Hsu 1983, pp. 275-87).

The overthrow of the *shogunate* as a part of the Meiji Restoration of 1868 replaced the military aristocracy, the *samurai*, by a new configuration of political and economic forces. In fact, decentralized Japanese feudalism was replaced by a modern centralized state that was ruled by a political oligarchy. With the removal of feudalism, the *han* system was eliminated and the *samurai* were stripped of their predominance. This is illuminated by the introduction of the new conscript system in

1870-73. The emasculation of the *samurai* was further symbolized by the government decision in 1876 not to permit the *samurai* to wear swords at all. Yet, the Meiji government realized that a total discrimination against the *samurai* would elicit outbursts of discontent, as happened in the Hagi and Satsuma rebellions in 1876-77, and so challenge the new power elite. That is why a variety of methods were used to absorb the *samurai* into the new society, though only with partial success (Hunter 1989, pp. 269-70).

The Meiji period did not mean only the restoration of the Emperor, but also the breakthrough of a new ruling class. This marked a terminal point in the long-term relative decline of the *samurai* as a social class. In the midst of change there was also continuity. Japan of the late nineteenth century was an agrarian nation and that is why the rural landowners remained an important pillar of the ruling class.

Bureaucracy emerged as the central force in the Meiji state, and it become an intermediary between other social forces. Many bureaucrats came from the *samurai* class, thus also providing continuity between traditional and modern Japan. It has even been suggested that the basic nature of the Meiji Restoration was the *samurai*-zation of the lower echelons of society which guaranteed the prevalence of loyalty and obedience among them (Lehmann 1982, pp. 158-9). The change of power did not abolish the traditional Confucian values, and they remained an indivisible part of the Meiji society (Marshall 1967, pp. 9-11).

The Japanese bureaucracy was institutionalized early on in the process of restoration. The present powerful MITI was established in 1881 as a part of the Ministry of Agriculture and Commerce. In 1885 the Ministry of Communication was created to take care of postal and telegraph services. In the early Meiji period the ministries were established primarily to prop up the state structure and to guide the forced industrialization of the economy. The bureaucracy thus became a linchpin in the development of Japan's industrial modernization which, right from the beginning, had strong military overtones (Johnson 1982).

Nationalism became a pervasive ideology in the Japanese society. It was assertive in advocating political unity and demanding for Japan a strong place in the international system (Lehmann 1982, pp. 155-6). This is reflected in the leading theme of the Restoration: *fukoku kyohei* (rich country, strongly armed). The new ruling coalition took the task of spreading the ideas of modernity and national unity to the people. The most important instruments in this effort were the educational system and the conscript army (Halliday 1975, pp. 34-8; Beasley 1982, pp. 112, 139-40). The Meiji education system and, in particular, the Education Act of 1872 was "part and parcel of the *fukoku-kyohei* ambition" (Lehmann 1982, pp. 259-65).

In order to succeed in the modernizing mission, the ruling coalition wanted to separate the state from party politics and, in that way, to keep it strong and autonomous. The state was invested with the task to "strengthen Japan as an independent nation *vis-à-vis* the outside world; and redistributing it internally to consolidate the new ruling bloc, whose political survival in the new global context depended on economic transformation" (Halliday 1975, p. 22). The strong state-bureaucracy has continued to characterize the Japanese society until today. Such a concentration of power often fuels popular demands to share power in a more equitable manner.

The Meiji Restoration initiated in Japan's political history a deep-rooted conflict between the popular political mobilization and the bureaucratic-authoritarian rule. The Restoration increased the powers of the Emperor, but in many respects his position was still ambiguous. In a way, the Emperor was made a central symbol, but not an effective ruler. The bureaucrats accumulated political power in the name of the Emperor to build a strong national state. This process did not progress without tensions, however. The transformation from feudalism to bureaucratic nationalism not only altered the structure of entitlements and privileges, but also created a variety of discontents and catalysed active demands for "popular rights" (Beasley 1982, pp. 120-2).

The new ruling coalition was successful in the consolidation of its power, although the suppression of the feudal opposition took quite a while. The military victory of the government over Saigo in the Satsuma rebellion in 1877 was decisive in this respect. The *samurai*, following the traditional individual fighting tactics, were not able to match the modern methods of warfare practised by the peasant conscript army. After its victory in the civil war the government could concentrate on furthering economic development and converting Japan from a subordinate agrarian country to an industrial power of regional and even global consequence.

Industrial Development

The Meiji Restoration was motivated by fear of the Western economic and military superiority. The national resentment was further fuelled by the unequal treaty situation that persisted to the closing years of the nineteenth century. The unequal treaties deprived Japan of any genuine opportunity to pursue a general policy of import-substituting industrialization behind protective tariffs. That is why it had to start to specialize economically right from the beginning (Halliday 1975, pp. 52-3). One of the sectors in which Japan specialized was the shipbuilding industry, which, much as it did in Britain, played a major role during the take-off period of Japan's economic growth in 1885-1905 (Rostow 1978, pp. 423-5).

The import-substituting development would not have been feasible without the intervention of the state to establish foundations for industrial development. Government was needed to accumulate funds which were largely derived from the farmers' savings (Beasley 1982, pp. 141-3). Another important reason for state intervention was that the unequal treaties imposed by Britain and the United States in the late 1850s and the early 1860s on Japan deprived her until the end of the nineteenth century of the ability to protect the nascent industries by tariffs. As tariff protection became possibly only after 1891, and more significantly from 1911 onwards, the state had to become directly involved in setting up strategic industries (Sen 1984, pp. 128-9).

In spite of the breakthrough of an industrial revolution in Japan, agriculture remained the most important branch of the economy and had much influence on the shape of society. In Japan agriculture had a visible role in economic modernization; in fact, "economic modernization began, not with the factory, but with the farm . . . agriculture generated much of the savings that supported private and public investment in the Meiji industry" (Lockwood 1954, pp. 25-7; Beasley 1982, pp. 141-3; Hayashi 1990, pp. 82-92). The central role of agriculture and its institutional and technological reforms in underpinning industrial development justifies a parallel between Meiji Japan and South Korea, and potentially China, after World War II. In both Japan and South Korea the modernization of agriculture helped to achieve, in their own contexts, remarkable rates of economic growth.

The Meiji reformers were mercantilists in that they regarded the chief objective of the economic policy to be the increase of national power. Yet, from the 1880s on private enterprise was permitted and even encouraged in many fields, such as shipping and light industry, as the most direct way to wealth. This dualistic policy can be traced back to a combination of the focus on national power and vulnerability and the impact of liberal economic principles (Lockwood 1954, pp. 504-5). The stress on private enterprise in the process of industrialization, however, also produced disappointments.

Initially, the traditional merchants were unwilling to adopt novel practices and were gradually replaced by the new industrialists. Yet they, also, were too weak to take the necessary risks, particularly in heavy industry. The relative weakness of the private industrial and merchant class was connected with the prevailing attitude of the Tokugawa period that considered economic activities demeaning and unfit for a member of the ruling class. The stigma was removed, however, from the industrial and commercial activities by the end of the 1880s when the idea of the nationalist businessman emerged. Private business was justified by its contribution to the national strength and well-being (Hunter 1989, pp. 114-16).

To strengthen private business, the Ministry of Industry, founded in 1870, started to establish pilot plants as a model for entrepreneurs, and also became involved, despite the financial crunch of the state in the 1870s, in the promotion of industry in general. The industrialization process was based, to a large degree, on imitation. Fact-finding missions, such as Iwakura mission, were dispatched to the West to learn new technical and organizational skills. The number of foreigners in Japan also increased rapidly, though remaining small in absolute figures, and brought new ideas and skills to the country. This phase of state intervention in the industrial development in the early 1870s is known as *shokusan kogyo* (production and industry) (Hirschmeier and Yui 1975, p. 80).

State-directed enterprises were most visible in heavy industries: mining, shipbuilding, railways, machinery, construction and armament. Government intervention emphasized the promotion of communication and transportation on the one hand and the military-related industrial production on the other (Hirschmeier and Yui 1975, pp. 86-8). National coherence and power were, in the best tradition of strategic mercantilism, the main objectives of the industrial policy of Meiji Japan.

Private initiative remained dominant in light industry such as silk and cotton spinning. The Japanese experience supports James K. Kurth's (1979) thesis that in late-industrializing countries, only the state can raise the significant amounts of capital needed to establish the heavy industry. In light industry the need for capital is less pronounced, and short-term rewards of investment greater; as a consequence, private companies are better able to succeed. In Japan, the situation in the organization and financial arrangements of the silk industry testifies to the validity of this observation (Allen 1962, pp. 68-9).

According to Kurth (1979), the economic priority placed on state-run heavy industry usually correlates with the prevalence of bureaucracy and an authoritarian political system. Heavy industry and a strong public sector are interconnected, and they tend to prop up military strength as the third tip of this iron triangle. Thus, a "hard core" of an upwardly-mobile country develops.

The direct participation of the state in the industrial development of the Meiji Japan was not intended to become permanent, however. After the early 1880s the state intervention in the civilian industry gradually withered away and the "state capitalism in the sense of public ownership played a declining role in prewar Japan until its revival in the war economy of the late thirties" (Lockwood 1954, pp. 507-8). The turning point was the sale, often at discount prices, of the government's pilot plants to those merchants, *seisho*, who had political connections. The new entrepreneurs achieved almost a monopoly position in critical industries and laid down the foundations for the *zaibatsu*, including the House of Mitsui and the Mitsubishi Company (Hirschmeier and Yui 1975, pp. 96-9, 132-42; Beasley 1982, pp. 146-9).

However, the state did not give up its role in industrial operations altogether. Largely for military reasons, the government established in 1896 the Yawata Iron Works and soon thereafter nationalized all the trunk railways. In general, the state retained its direct control over arsenals and military-related production, while the *zaibatsu* assumed the control of the civilian industries. A kind of co-operative division of labour emerged in which the state had the final say in the military industries, while the *zaibatsu* took over and controlled the civilian market.

One reason for the state's promotion of the division of labour between the public and the private sector was its financial crisis; the capital-poor state wanted to get rid of its civilian industrial commitments and channel this money for power-related investments, including direct military spending. The switch to the selective participation of the Japanese state in industrial development, coinciding with its efforts to strengthen the military as a spearhead of national development, can thus be explained by the lack of capital (Lockwood 1954, pp. 507-9; Halliday 1975, pp. 59-60).

The Japanese Military

It has been suggested that "the role of the military in Japan's transformation to modernity was pervasive". This observation is based on the role of the military sponsoring heavy industry, for which the state remained by far the most important client (Lehmann 1982, pp. 268-9). The triangle of the state, the military and heavy industry shaped the path of Japan's economic development from the 1880s on.

After Commodore Perry's visit, the expansion of foreign influence gave rise in Japan to the deep-seated perception of Western threat and to policy debates on how best to avert it. The *bakufu* opted for opening the country as a tactical move to accumulate new strength and to expel the foreigners, and saw the acquisition of military capabilities in the 1850s and the 1860s as a countervailing strategy to Western influence. Western military doctrines were studied and weapons purchased, but at the same time foundries, arsenals and shipyards were constructed to establish a base for domestic military industry (Beckmann 1962, pp. 248-9).

In the 1850s the leading domains, such as Saga and Satsuma, established ironworks to produce cannons; in 1843-67 346 cannons were produced in total but most of them were of relatively low quality. In addition to armaments manufacturing, the leading domains were determined to expand shipbuilding, in part by Dutch assistance. The main purpose was to protect the coasts, but gradually the idea of building an ocean-going navy started to grow. The acquisition of Western military technology by the domains was based on the local initiative of the *han* lords: "they began with the premise that Japan had to have greater military capability, which would be acquired by possessing steamships and weapons that could resist the armed forces of the Western powers" (Mitsukuni 1985, pp. 194-5; Hayashi 1990, pp. 93-4).

By Western standards there was, indeed, much to be done to strengthen the military. In particular after the Crimean War the application of industrial principles to weapons production and warfare became the international norm (McNeill 1982). The industrialization of warfare had extensive international repercussions, and Japan did not avoid its impact. In the middle of the nineteenth century military technology in East Asia was pretty much the same as it had been during the preceding two centuries. The Opium War of 1839-42 showed in a concrete manner that militarily China could not resist the Western military organization and technology (Hacker 1977, pp. 47-8 and Hsu 1983, pp. 192-3).

For several reasons Japan started its military modernization earlier than China; for example, it perceived the Western threat more seriously and was also more inclined to seek equality with other powers. To achieve this objective, the Japanese repeatedly suggested that their country should follow the development model of another insular nation, England (Jansen 1984, pp. 63-4). Indeed, the Royal Navy had a relatively strong influence on the development of the Japanese navy and contributed to the instruction in the Japanese Naval Academy, the *Kaigun Daigakko*, established in 1888. Conversely, the organization of Japanese society was promoted, particularly after the defeat of Russia in 1904-05, as a model which Britain should adopt in order to overcome its weaknesses (Searle 1971, pp. 57-9).

During the Tokugawa period the Japanese navy was influenced primarily by its Dutch and French counterparts. In 1870 it was ordered that the navy should follow the British and the army the French pattern. The Douglas Mission from the Royal Navy in 1873 was decisive in cementing the ties with the Japanese navy, which also acquired British ships. As a consequence, "the rapid progress of naval technology allowed the infant Japanese navy to acquire new naval technology on an equal footing with other naval powers" (Ikeda 1988, p. 182). In the naval field Japan's rise was predicated on its alignment, since 1902, with the leading naval power of the era, Great Britain.

In the army, the French influence was dominant initially, while in the late Meiji period the German role became conspicuous. The military organization and education was modelled along the German lines and with the help of German military advisers, largely because of the tireless work of Taro Katsura who studied in Germany in 1871-78. An important reason for the Japanese interest in the German army was the latter's victorious conduct of the Franco-Prussian war in 1870-71. The German influence in the Japanese army was greatest in its organizational structure, as it was recognized that "an army's effectiveness rested on organization as much on weapons" (Beasley 1972, p. 412). In practical terms, the most important reforms were the introduction of the German-style conscription system in 1873 and the separation of the General Staff from the War Ministry (Miyake 1977, pp. 159-61).

The Japanese army reforms had profound social and political implications. In Japan, as in Germany, a chief function of the army was to consolidate the national state and to bind the people to the military establishment. Conscription and education were the main means by which the Japanese government indoctrinated the new generations in its own ideology (Beasley 1982, p. 112). The coercive apparatus of the state in both Japan and Germany was linked to the head of state, whether the Kaiser or the Emperor, by the direct chain of command (on the organization of the Meiji armed forces, see Fugushima 1966, pp. 198-205).

In that way the army was insulated from the expanding popular rights movement and the services became the main pillars of the imperial rule. This meant that the "army and the navy were to be regarded as personal servants of the Throne, that they were to serve as the ultimate check against any political movement which might lead in the direction of a republican or constitutional government that would compromise the absolute authority of the emperor" (Crowley 1974, pp. 9-11; Lehmann 1982, pp. 270-2; Hunter 1989, pp. 272-3). Similarly, the Meiji police system was based on the military model, imported from France and Germany, and served the function of internal pacification against the democratic demands of emerging political movements (Westney 1987, pp. 60-2).

In the late nineteenth century there was in Japan a widespread perception that it was living in a Darwinian world where territorial imperialism of great powers was the hallmark of the era. This definition of the global situation justified the prescription that Japan should also start expanding territorially, in order to defend its interests against the spread of the British and Russian imperialism in particular. The call for expansion originated primarily with the army leaders (Jansen 1984, pp. 66-7). However, Japanese expansion before World War I was also supported by other interest groups, such as business leaders, which made the policy less coherent and deliberate than one might have expected.

With the progress of the Meiji period the notion of the businessman as a warrior developed: rather than making profit the businessman should serve the nation. In this context, "service to the nation meant contributing to the building of a rich country and a strong military" (Marshall 1967, pp. 46-50). This kind of thinking, spreading on a national scale, created an expansive morale which underpinned Japan's quest for economic and military dominance (Kennedy 1987, p. 208).

Industrial modernization was considered important in its own right, but it was also regarded as necessary for the build-up of military power. In this spirit, the members of the Iwakura mission to Europe and North America in 1871-73 were alerted to observe the military organization and equipment in the countries they visited. In general, the Iwakura mission had the task of collecting information and experience that would help Japan to carry through an internal reform with the objective of restoring her diplomatic and military equality with the Western powers (Beasley 1972, pp. 368-71; Lehmann 1982, pp. 186-7).

As pointed out earlier, Japan's decision to opt for an integrated military-industrial strategy of development was based on heavy state intervention in the economy that probably contributed to its territorial expansion and wars (Hacker 1977, pp. 52-3). The impact of state intervention and the intermingling of civilian and military interests in Japan's industrialization surfaces in its railway programmes in the late nineteenth century. In the beginning, there was a debate on whether railways only engender unnecessary costs or whether they are necessary spearheads of strategic mobility, both commercial and military. The first railway was built in Japan in 1872 by the state, but by the early 1890s the railways were gradually privatized. In 1906 they were again nationalized, both on economic and strategic grounds. Military interests alone shaped the early railways programmes of Japan. Gradually, however, they coalesced with the objectives of the railway technocrats, and technological compatibility and consistency became the common denominator of military and civilian interests (Watarai 1915; Beasley 1972, pp. 355-8; Hayashi 1990, pp. 123-5).

The surge of Japanese nationalism towards the end of the nineteenth century was closely connected with militarism and territorial expansionism which resulted in a series of wars in the turn of the century. Until 1894 Japanese expansionism advanced without outright war, but then its bellicosity became manifest. In 1894-95 Japan waged war with China, in 1900-1 it took part in the suppression of the Boxer rebellion, in 1904-5 it defeated Russia and in 1910 Korea was annexed. By then Japan had become the dominant regional power in North-East Asia, largely by the force of its modern military weapons, but also by its economic strength and expansion.

Japan's expansion to North-East Asia was motivated largely by strategic considerations to contain the Russian expansionism there. This objective also underpinned the Anglo-Japanese co-operation which materialized in a bilateral alliance in 1902. Strategic and economic goals seldom contradict each other; rather they are often mutually supportive. In the increasingly competitive economic relations between the major powers in the 1890s, Japan also felt the need to expand its exports. This was motivated by the need to strengthen Japanese control over the Asian markets and to earn foreign exchange to finance the imports of raw materials, producer durables and armaments. Military and economic aspects of the Meiji expansionism became intertwined with each other (Duus 1984, pp. 131-7; Crowley 1974, pp. 15-21).

Japan's overall military expansion at the turn of the century was visible; yet it was constrained by its military weakness in relation to the Western powers. As to China, however, Japan was technologically and military preponderant, and the growing differential of military power facilitated an expansionist policy in that direction (Halliday 1975, p. 85). In 1896 Japan initiated a ten-year armament programme by which the army and navy were considerably expanded. As a result of the programme, Japan became self-sufficient in naval armaments, despite the increase in the number of ships. It was made militarily strong enough to face any adversary operating in the region, except for the British fleet (Crowley 1974, p. 19; Beasley 1982, pp. 164-5). This was not a problem, however, as Japan and Britain had agreed on mutual co-operation and division of labour in the Far East.

The military expansion programme pushed military spending upwards. In 1894-1900 the share of military spending of the total government expenditure slowly increased and varied between 15.6 and 21.5 per cent. In 1901 the share jumped to 28.4 per cent and reached 83.2 per cent in 1905 during the Russo-Japanese war. After that the share of military spending declined, but remained at a high level of some 45 per cent until 1913 (Banks 1982, p. 117). The decision to step up military spending seriously drained Japan's financial resources. In order to avoid a fiscal crunch the state had both to privatize state-owned industries and start borrowing money from the Western money markets (Lockwood 1954, pp. 250-3). Japan's militarization, though it was not the sole reason, forced the country into foreign debt.

By the turn of the nineteenth century the "old militarism" of Japan had become entrenched in its society and the country itself had become a major military and political power in Asia (Hoyt 1985, pp. 61-5). In Japan, international strategic competition, in particular with Russia, had justified the augmentation of national military capabilities. On the other hand, the heavy industrialization strategy permitted Japan to acquire military power which served her expansionist policies in Asia before World War I.

Military Industry

Japan's military industry emerged during the last years of the Tokugawa regime, but its sustained expansion was fomented by the Meiji Restoration. The strong involvement of the Meiji oligarchy in the promotion of military industries was motivated by several reasons. First, it wanted to create a strong country, and for such a purpose a modern army and navy was a necessity. They could not be created without establishing, in turn, strategic industries to support the military institutions. Once this policy was chosen there was really no other alternative than to involve the state, which had to "develop military industries - arsenals, shipyards and mining - because of the lack of entrepreneurs, pre-capitalist level of technology and modest capital accumulation" (Norman 1940, p. 120; see also Allen 1962, p. 79).

The Meiji Japan was typically a latecomer country which chose the catch-up policy of industrialization. This is reflected in the fact that in Japan heavy industry was developed, in effect, before light industry, and almost exclusively for military purposes. Only at the turn of the nineteenth century did the textile industry start to expand and complement the heavy industry (Ando 1966, p. 118; Halliday 1975, pp. 57-8). The priority given to heavy military industry is illustrated by its access to steam power, where as the private sector had to be content with human and water power (Hayashi 1990, p. 40).

From the beginning, the military industries were an essential part of heavy industry and provided a model for other industries. The government retained control of military industries even after the 1880s when most other industries were privatized. In effect, the release of public resources by the privatization of companies strengthened the military industries, as the state could more effectively support them. Furthermore, the privatization of civilian industries did not mean that their linkages with the state were severed; on the contrary, they remained rather close (Norman 1940, pp. 128-31; Halliday 1975, pp. 59-60).

The Meiji government established arsenals, shipbuilding yards and explosives factories, which, in turn, launched a considerable number of armament projects (for lists of factories and projects, see Ando 1966, pp. 115-16 and 130-1). By the late 1870s four main arsenals were established. The army arsenals were located in Tokyo and Osaka and produced small arms, ammunition and, by the middle of the 1880s, artillery and shells. They were advised by Belgian, French and German engineers and employed in 1884 about 3000 workers. The navy arsenals were located in Yokosuka and Tsukij and concentrated mostly on naval cannons and metallurgical technology (Yamamura 1977, pp. 114-15).

Japan was chronically dependent on imported iron and steel. The *bakufu* had been unable to launch a viable steel industry, and most of the country's needs were met by imports from abroad. The *bakufu* initiated the Yokosuka and Nagasaki Ironworks which were built to construct ships. However, they had to import all the machines and equipment needed and the work was supervised by foreign engineers (Mitsukuni 1985, pp. 196-8). There was "clearly, a big gap between the aims of the shogunal regime and the demand of modern technology". Furthermore, the shogunate had built too rigid a society to be able to develop and absorb modern technologies (Hayashi 1990, p. 103).

Facing such a legacy from the Tokugawa period, the Meiji rulers systematically embarked upon the promotion of the iron and steel industry. The main objective was to provide materials for the arsenals and shipbuilding industry both during the peace and, in particular, during the war (Ando 1966, pp. 120-3). There is conflicting evidence on the technological level and economic contribution of Japan's shipyards and engineering industry. This issue is critical because these branches were dominated in Meiji Japan by military production, which has been supposed to have had positive spin-off effects in the economy.

On the one hand, it has been observed that by the turn of the century "shipbuilding and engine manufacture had caught up with the world levels and had even surpassed them" (Ando 1966, pp. 125-7). On the other hand, it has been suggested that shipbuilding and engineering were, by the standards of Western powers, quite unimpressive until World War I, and were largely dependent on foreign imports (Allen 1962, pp. 82-3).

In weighing the arguments, one should not confuse Japan's external economic position with its internal dynamics. Before World War I, Japan's share of the world manufacturing output was miniscule. In total industrial potential it could only be compared with Italy, the weakest of the major powers, and in iron/steel production Japan even lagged behind her. In 1901 the standard bearer of the Japanese iron and steel industry, the Yawata Steel Works, produced less than one per cent of the output of US Steel (Kennedy 1987, pp. 200-2; Hayashi 1990, p. 98).

The delayed development of Japan's industry prompted the Meiji rulers, painfully aware of the underdevelopment of their country, to prop up the strategic industries. As I have repeatedly pointed out, state intervention was the main remedy used to eradicate the remnants of feudalism and to industrialize Japan. The impact of the state can be seen in the fact that in 1897 about one-half of the factories were government-owned and they consumed two-thirds of the total horsepower (Halliday 1975, pp. 58-9).

The history of Japan's iron and steel industry suggests how difficult the onset of a modern industry in a semi-developed country can be. It took two decades, after a series of initial failures, before Kamaishi Ironworks could produce, by the middle of the 1890s, a high-quality iron usable for military purposes. Its capacity was so limited, however, that the importation of iron and steel had to be continued. Naturally, the technology and organization of production had to be improved as well. This task was assigned to the state-owned Yawata Steelworks whose establishment had been called for by the military ever since the 1880s.

Yawata Steelworks, started in 1896, was developed by a German company, with disappointing results. In about 1910 the development of Yawata, increasingly done by Japanese experts, had reached the necessary standards of technological competence required at that time and made a contribution to Japan's military capability. Yet the mill still could not satisfy the demand created by expanding military production and the railway boom, and the importation of steel was continued (Yamamura 1977, pp. 125-7; Hayashi 1990, pp. 94-9).

In the shipbuilding industry a kind of interdependent division of labour emerged by the 1880s between the government and the private entrepreneurs. Some of the government shipyards (Nagasaki, Kobe, Uraga and Ishikawa) were privatized and new private yards, such as Osaka Iron Works and the Ono Shipbuilding Company, were established. However, their output remained small until the early twentieth century, and vessels had to be imported (Allen 1962, p. 82). The expansion of shipbuilding started in earnest in 1896 when the Navigation Subsidy Act and the Shipbuilding Encouragement Act were passed. Both Acts were intended - succesfully one might add

- to divert shipbuilding to domestic yards to meet the growing demand for ships in the merchant fleet (Sen 1984, pp. 132-4; Allen 1962, pp. 91-2).

The state-owned shipyards, most notably the Yokosuka yard, produced all the naval ships from 1874 to 1905, although their share declined to 73 per cent in 1906-15 (Ando 1966, p. 127). Had these yards been producing only for the navy, their industrial impact could probably be dismissed. The military arsenals and shipyards, however, spearheaded Japan's technological modernization from its initially primitive level of departure. They actively supported the private sector by providing, among other things, steam engines, various types of machinery and simple machine tools (Yamamura 1977, pp. 116-17). This evidence appears credible, although some critical remarks can be made about its validity in corroborating the basic argument (Rice 1977, pp. 136-7).

From the middle of the 1890s onwards Japan experienced a vigorous economic expansion; industrial production, in particular light industry, grew rapidly and became dependent on foreign markets. The heavy industry, especially the iron and steel production, also expanded; it did not reach an international market, however, but was limited to building the national economic and military foundation that supported international expansion in other fields (Beckmann 1965, pp. 338-41; Beasley 1982, pp. 165-6).

The growth of heavy industry during the Meiji era enhanced the Japanese self-confidence and, in that way, obviously encouraged expansion. Later on, the expansion of cotton manufacturing created a business-driven penetration in the Korean and other Asian markets (Duus 1984, pp. 151-4). In Meiji Japan, warfare seems to have created domestic discontinuities which fostered economic growth. From 1895 on, the victory in the Sino-Japanese war both expanded the production capabilities of arsenals and, more generally, pointed to the profitability of military activities (Yamamura 1977, p. 121; Duus 1984, p. 143).

Indeed, the Sino-Japanese and Russo-Japanese wars augmented the military-related technological capabilities in both state-owned and private companies by promoting the spread of know-how from the military to the civilian fields. In particular the Russo-Japanese war pushed the dissemination of modern technologies, such as machines and machine-tools, from large arsenals and shipyards to small companies. These companies were lifted to their feet by the war and continued their existence thereafter. The Russo-Japanese war also strengthened the private shipbuilding companies such as Ishikawajima, Kawasaki and Nagasaki (Yamamura 1977, pp. 120-5).

The Russo-Japanese war made Japan leap into the construction of big naval ships which were equal in quality and size to those of the Western naval powers. In that way Japan became a participant in the naval race that preceded World War I. In addition, the rapid increase in tonnage during the Russo-Japanese war permitted the diversion of new ships to civilian commercial uses on new routes to other Asian countries and, in that way, contributed to external economic expansion (Allen 1962, p. 92; Hirschmeier and Yui 1975, p. 147).

Conclusions

The Japanese experience gives rise to several general observations. In the technological context there is quite clear evidence that military industries had positive spin-off effects in the civilian sector. Armament production became a model for heavy industry which, to a large extent, was controlled by the state. This should not lead, however, to a simplified conclusion that the rapid pace of Japan's industrialization can be explained solely by state intervention, in particular in the military and non-military heavy industries. Nishikawa and Saito (1985, pp. 188-9) have pointed out that the distinction between centralism and decentralism matters more than that of government and private interests.

In effect, the public and private interests became strongly intertwined in the early industrialization of Japan. In heavy military industry the state dominated, though its prevalence decreased over time, while in light industry the private interests were stronger. In the intermediary sectors these two interests were intermingled. State intervention was dictated more by the need to raise capital than the intrinsic willingness of the Japanese policy-makers to steer industrial activities. The necessary capital had to be generated both by importing capital and by restricting domestic consumption; in so doing the Meiji government became an investment banker (Prestowitz 1988, pp. 105-7; Lockwood 1954, *passim*).

The centralization of the Japanese economy transferred power to the new bureaucracy which co-ordinated the fusion of public and private industry. "The merging of private and state capital, particularly in those branches of industry close to war economy, such as transport, steel and machine-making, gave new strength to the bureaucracy, placing it politically on an equal if not superior level to its partner, private monopoly capital" (Norman 1940, p. 133). The fusion of private and public interests was accompanied by the blurring of the organizational and technological distinction between military and non-military industries.

The strength of the centralized bureaucracy, co-operating with the private companies, was commensurate with the political control of society by the military (Crowley 1974, pp. 21-2). The army and the navy could not dictate their procurement programmes, but they were under relatively strict political supervision. In policy-making, this permitted consideration of the balance between economic costs and benefits of the military industrialization. The role of bureaucracy gives some indication that it was not only technology that contributed to Japan's modernization, but also its social organization. This was obviously the case within the military establishment as well: "an army's effectiveness rested on organization as much as on weapons" (Beasley 1972, p. 413).

Spin-off processes may either develop by their own momentum or be built in the economic system by political guidance. In Japan, the merger of public and private interests was obviously conducive to the spin-off process between the military and civilian industries. State intervention fostered new industries, especially heavy industries, while the market privatized some of the companies and disseminated new technologies. In fact, the selective introduction of new technologies to the military sector and their spread to the private industries may have been in the Japanese case the most significant spin-off process (Yamamura 1977, pp. 133-5).

Closely related to that was the introduction of technology consisting of assembled and interchangeable parts from the West. Such components could be more easily produced in a semi-developed economy like Japan; hence the indigenization of technology progressed. This development was particularly important in the manufacturing of small arms where standardization was important both for independent and flexible production and for effective military operations (Hayashi 1990, p. 104). The introduction of interchangeable parts into military industries paved the way for the adoption of a similar technique in the production of sewing machines, watches and bicycles.

In Japan, the public-private linkages and the targeting of foreign technologies gave rise to a dual structure of the economy. This was a result of the initial development gap between Japan and the leading Western powers. The strong state was able to acquire advanced technology abroad and use it to strengthen its own position in relation to the nation's peripheries. The division of the Japanese economy into modern and traditional sectors and the control of peripheries were facilitated by the "ability of its leaders to convert the ideological function to modern purposes", that is, domain loyalty was converted into nationalism (Rozman 1990, pp. 183-4). The economic duality was also associated with the selective utilization of foreign technology. The Meiji government pursued an explicit policy of technological autonomy. It was promoted by hiring well-paid foreign experts only in the most critical sectors of the economy that had been accorded political priority. In addition, these experts were sent back as soon as their skills had been absorbed locally. The process of assimilating foreign technologies was supported by investing in the domestic training of engineers (Ando 1966, p. 134; Beasley 1982, p. 144; Hunter 1989, pp. 109-10).

The Meiji government wanted to avoid one-sided dependence on any of the major Western powers. As a consequence, none of them was taken as the sole model of development (Hunter 1989, pp. 20-1). In that way Japan circumvented roadblocks to the indigenization of foreign technology that unilateral dependencies might have created. Yet the dependence on some imported inputs, such as raw materials and machine tools, could not be avoided altogether (Ando 1966, p. 133). The positive spin-offs from military production to the civilian economy were thus mediated by the policy of the Meiji government in the context of the prevailing structure of Japanese society.

To a degree, the positive linkages were also facilitated in pre-World War I Japan by dualism not only between government vs. private, but also between big vs. small and central vs. peripheral. In fact, the socio-economic polarization appears in most upwardly mobile nations catching up other powers further up the hierarchy. The potential for economic and military expansion is accumulated by exploiting the domestic peripheries, whether social or geographical. Over time, the new capabilities are expected to trickle down and to create a broad-based and equitable pattern of development.

The Japanese militarization and expansion took a more active and sustained path from the middle of the 1890s onwards (Lehmann 1982, pp. 308-9). The wars waged by Japan against China and Russia reinforced the pattern of military-based industrialization initiated in the last years of the Tokugawa rule. The wars naturally stepped up military development and production and in the short run emphasized the public sector. After the war, many arms manufacturers turned to the production of civilian goods, as did those gunsmiths who started manufacturing bicycles after the Russo-Japanese war (Allen 1962, p. 85). Thus, over the long term, wars may have strengthened the private sector and contributed to the private-public dualism characteristic of the Japanese economy.

The military factor was deeply embedded in the pattern of Japanese development, in particular in its statist dimension. The centrality of state was carried over to the interwar period when the state institutions and civilian bureaucracy co-operated with the military in developing an authoritarian "statist solution" (Garon 1987, pp. 187-227). The carry-over effect was also visible in the economic and technological linkages between military production and civilian applications, which tended to be positive in the interwar years as well (Kahler 1988).

Japan's zig-zag rise to its present economic strength was stimulated initially, after the Meiji Restoration, by the military programmes aiming at national strength and technological autonomy. The short-term economic benefits were followed, however, by adverse consequences over the long term. Extracting capital for public military and civilian investment, both from domestic private investment and from abroad, apparently fuelled industrialization and economic growth. On the downside, small-scale industry suffered from shortage of capital, and there were few resources to develop the peripheries such as Hokkaido and to improve the education and social welfare of the citizenry (Lockwood 1954, pp. 291-3).

The priority accorded to the public sector and investment, under the aegis of a strong bureaucracy, centralized decision-making and undermined democratic control, and in that way made the leap to war easier. The price of forced industrialization was high, both for Japan and its Asian neighbours. This is tragic, since the long-term economic benefits could probably have been achieved by an alternative path of development which would have utilized more effectively the innovative and entrepreneurial capacities of the Japanese people. This argument is borne out by the experience of the post-World War II period: the Japanese economy has expanded without the military stimulant, which has been limited by internal and external political constraints.

Chapter 3
Military Production and British Decline

The Decline of Britain

The first phase in the relative economic decline of Britain has usually been timed to the downswing of a long wave in 1873-96 when both prices and profits fell. This downswing did not affect all the European economies equally. While the German and US economies, for instance, continued to grow in quite a vigorous, albeit internally imbalanced manner, the British economy, and particularly its agricultural sector, suffered seriously from the global stagnation. The British growth rates were flat from the 1860s through the 1870s. In the early 1890s both the United States and Germany passed Britain in the production of steel. In general, the immediate benefits of the first industrial revolution wore off and the British economy was not able to switch to a new technological and institutional gear (Hobsbawm 1968, pp. 103-6; Thompson 1990, p.226).

The British situation reflects a general trend; the downswing of a long cycle has a stronger negative impact on the economic growth of declining powers than on those of the upwardly mobile powers. During the downswing the economic and political dimensions of international power are merged with each other, while during the upswing market forces are more autonomous. In the downswing the challengers to the dominant country use their state power to prop up economic performance, especially in the emerging key industries.

There is considerable agreement among historians on the approximate starting point of the relative British decline. Paul M. Kennedy (1981, pp. 20-7) dates the zenith of the British power to the mid-1860s when Britain's relative industrial capability started to decline quite rapidly and the centre of technological innovation switched especially to Germany and the United States. In a similar vein, Brian Porter (1983, pp. 34-6) dates the beginning of the British economic decline to 1873, the first year of the first Great Depression. William R. Thompson (1990, p. 226) deviates somewhat from this consensus by suggesting that the British "decline process was discernible as early as in the mid-nineteenth century and perhaps even a little earlier". On the other hand, Andrew Gamble (1990, pp. 73-5) considers the period 1880-1914 as "the challenge to the empire" and in that sense as the first phase in the British decline.

From 1870 to 1913 the British economy grew by some 1.6 per cent per annum, while the comparable growth rates of Germany and the United States in the economy as a whole and in industry were two to three times higher (Friedberg 1988, pp. 25-6; Pollard 1989, pp. 12-13). The US and German growth rates exceeded the British ones, sometimes by a considerable margin, in all the leading sectors such as iron, steel, railways and chemicals (Thompson 1990, pp. 228-9). Longitudinally, it may be observed that in 1873-1913 the annual average growth rate of the British GDP was 1.8

per cent, while in the preceding and succeeding periods of comparable length the growth rate averaged 2.2 per cent (Matthews, Feinstein and Odling-Smee 1982, p. 22).

The British decline became manifest on a number of economic dimensions. Its labour productivity in industry grew very little from the 1880s onwards and the total factor productivity performed even more badly, especially in 1900-7. In fact, in 1873-1913 there was no increase in the total factor productivity at all; the modest growth in productivity can be explained by the increases in factor input alone (Mathias 1983, pp. 371-2). This picture is confirmed by other studies which show that in 1873-1913 the annual percentage growth rate of the total factor productivity was 0.5 per cent, an all time low in the British economic experience since 1856 (Matthews, Feinstein and Odling-Smee 1982, p. 532).

The slowdown in the growth of productivity was, in part, engendered by the economic stagnation itself. The funds for investment in new export-oriented industries dried up as the profits were squeezed by declining prices and stagnant volumes (Mathias 1983, p. 366). The adverse impact of the long depression on agriculture also slowed down the productivity growth, as did the emerging technology gap between Britain and its main competitors (Matthews, Feinstein and Odling-Smee 1982, pp. 533-7). The British economy faced, in other words, a vicious circle; it became a prisoner of the downswing of the international economic cycle and its own decline.

The slow growth of productivity was associated with the loss of technological leadership and with the failure to invest funds in the renewal of domestic industry (cf. Wiener 1981, pp. 29-30). When the industrial structure of the previous long wave aged, its constitutient units became, relatively speaking, less innovative and productive. James Kurth, in particular, has emphasized how the successive phases of the British industries reached their saturation point and experienced diminishing returns. The steel industry expanded to new areas of production, which helped for a while, but ultimately ended up in an economic depression. The naval procurement was used from the middle of the 1880s as counter-cyclical policy. The British steel industry had been weakened in relative terms, however, to the extent that it was not capable of reconquering the market and establishing an alternative political and economic order (Kurth 1979, pp. 15-19).

British industry was also slow to make progress in new and promising industrial areas such as the chemical industry, electrical engineering and the motor car industry. As a consequence, the British export performance gradually weakened, particularly in the manufacturing sector. This contributed, in turn, to the growing trade deficit and to structural imbalances in the economy (Kirby 1981, pp. 2-3, 11; Sandberg 1981, pp. 109-14; Mathias 1983, pp. 234-5, 378-85).

From the strategic point of view the most significant development was the decline of the British share of production and exports in such pivotal sectors as transport equipment, metals and machinery. The new dominance of Germany and the United States in the export market can be seen in the fact that in 1890-1913 nearly one-half of the growth in exports of manufactured goods by industrialized countries originated from these two economic centres. Yet, in 1913 Britain was the largest exporter in the world, although her relative position in manufactured exports was weaker than in the export trade overall. Britain was more dependent than other powers on manufactured exports; their share of manufactured output exceeded 40 per cent in Britain, but was only 5 per cent in the United States and some 30 per cent in Germany (Aldcroft 1968, pp. 19-21; Pollard 1989, pp. 14-15).

Internally consistent with this shift from the manufactured to non-manufactured exports is the redirection of British exports from the markets of industrialized countries to colonies, in particular to its own empire. Access to the colonial markets was easier in that commercial operations there could be politically encouraged and steered (Sen 1984, pp. 163-70). Yet even in many primary producing countries, except for semi-industrial ones, the US and German exporters were able to increase their market shares at the expense of the British companies (Aldcroft 1968, pp. 19-20).

The foreign trade of Britain was marked by large deficits for decades before World War I. In practice, the imbalance in the current account could be rectified only by the export of services such as finance, shipping and insurance, globally dominated by the British banks and companies. The export of services was particularly profitable in the non-European regions where services related to commerce and direct investment were poorly developed (Mathias 1983, pp. 277-282). Financial, shipping and insurance services became British industries in their own right and underpinned interest groups which, along with exporters of goods, defended the continuation of free trade policies against the tariff reform movement. The reaching out of the financial institutions to the global marketplace led to neglect of the domestic industry and to the shortage of risk capital (Gourevitch 1986, pp. 76-83; O'Brien 1990, pp. 30-2).

The relative decline of Britain coincided with the industrial rise of the continental powers of Europe. David Landes rightly observes that:

> The period from 1850 to 1873 was Continental industry's coming-of-age. It was a period of unprecedentedly rapid growth . . . These were also years of technological maturation. They were marked in essence by the working-out on the Continent of those innovations that constitute the heart of Industrial Revolution and had been developed and diffused in Britain a generation or more earlier. (Landes 1981, p. 193).

A difference between Great Britain and the Continent was that in the former textiles were for long the leading sector, while in the latter heavy industry, integrated with machine building, dominated from the outset (Landes 1981, pp. 174-87). The difference in the industrial patterns became more pronounced by the turn of the century and is obviously connected with the differences in the national economic performance.

During the period of decelerated economic growth in 1873-97 the importance of the national factor in the world economy increased. State intervention became more pronounced, in particular in Germany, and propped up the capital-goods industry. The liberal model of British hegemony was not capable of strengthening its competitive capacity and defending its share in the European and North American markets. The British market share declined in those markets and it had to resort to the imperial market to counterbalance the US and German challenge (McMichael 1985, pp. 138-9).

Capital goods were at the core of the second industrial revolution which was also characterized by a more intense international competition and redistribution of economic power. These phenomena were interlinked: Britain lost the struggle for the control of the newest technologies and industries:

> By the 1880s a new balance of power was already emerging in the world economy, and Britain's capacity to remain its leading state and the guarantor of the conditions world-wide under which accumulation of capital could proceed became more and more precarious. British decline begins with the organisation of a world economy based upon the rise of modern industry on a truly world scale. The challenge posed to Britain by Germany and the United States was both commercial and military. (Gamble 1981, p. 53)

This development is well reflected in the iron and steel industry in which Britain lost much of its influence from the late 1870s to the mid-1890s. During that period German steel prices fell, relatively speaking, thanks to rapid growth in productivity, and, along with the United States, Germany increased its share in the world steel and iron market. (Allen 1979, pp. 912-913, 928; Landes 1981, pp. 215-19). In the iron and steel market the national factor, including state intervention and military interests, is of central importance, and as a result the British decline had far-reaching political consequences.

Though the signs of the British decline were visible by the end of the nineteenth century, its strengths were still formidable. Its colonial empire was huge, its navy clearly surpassed the naval capabilities of the primary challengers and it was the leading capital exporter. The City of London reigned supreme in the world of finances. While recognizing the relevance of these strengths in Britain's international position, Paul M. Kennedy also points to the downside. The spread of industrial capabilities and innovations from Britain to the rising powers helped them to utilize more effectively their indigenous resources and to equalize the development differential (Kennedy 1987, pp. 151-8, 224-32).

In a word, the relative economic decline of Britain should be traced to its weakening position in international competition rather than to the protectionism of other powers. The British decline was not only and not even primarily due to its decision to stick to free trade, nor to the rise of its competitors; it was also self-generated. This thesis is further supported by the fact that, in comparison with Germany and the United States "a higher proportion of Britain's trade in manufactures was concentrated in declining export sectors with a correspondingly lower proportion in the most rapidly expanding groups" (Aldcroft 1968, pp. 22-4). Theoretically, this conclusion is consistent also with the corporatist thesis that the British decline has been caused by the flawed character of its domestic regime of accumulation (Gamble 1990, pp. 83-4).

The financial predominance of the City also had its drawbacks. Britain became increasingly dependent on the world economy and, as a result, its freedom of choice was curtailed, especially since the balance in the current account was dependent on the exports of financial and other services. The emphasis laid on financial operations at the expense of productive investments and innovations developed a *rentier* mentality in the economy. The *rentiers* lived on the results - profits and savings - of the first industrial revolution (Hobsbawm 1968, pp. 97-8; Mathias 1983, p. 235). In other words, Britain's strengths were converted, to a degree, into weaknesses in the course of its relative decline.

Once the thesis on the relative economic decline of Britain is accepted, with appropriate empirical caveats (cf. Maddison 1982, p. 38), the next logical question is the role of military spending and production in this trend. Did the allocation of societal resources to military purposes undermine the investment of human, technical and financial resources to renew the British industry? Or was the decline due to the profound structural forces, divorced from political decisions, that operated in the economy and that possibly shaped the patterns of growth in military spending as well?

Military Strategy and Industry

Measured in terms of its share of GNP, British military spending remained rather constant, between 2 and 3 per cent, from the 1840s to the end of the nineteenth century. In fact, a slight decline is evident during this period, except for the increase caused by British involvement in the Crimean War in the 1850s. In the 1880s and the 1890s military expenditure as a proportion of GNP was relatively low, at 1.8 and 2.2 per cent, respectively (Rasler and Thompson 1988, p. 71).

In the decades preceding World War I, the figures for military share of the national budget up to 1913 also show a relatively stable spending pattern, except for the Boer War. In 1899-1902 this share jumped from a standard 35 per cent to 60 per cent and even more (Köhler 1980). Military spending as a percentage of GNP therefore also peaked at the turn of the century when it rose to around 6 per cent. The relative military burden decreased after the Boer War, but then started a slow climb to World War I (Rasler and Thompson 1988, p. 71).

These trends suggest that long-term economic fluctuations had little effect on variations in British military spending. This may be due both to the ability of other factors to account for the variations in military spending and to some doubt about the existence of any Kondratiev waves in the British economy (Solomou 1988, pp. 27-33; Mathias 1983, pp. 362-3). An alternative to the long-cycle theory in explaining the relative level of military spending is that Britain's military policy and priorities were shaped more by its hegemonic and colonial position in the world.

British expansion was directed to the sea lanes and overseas colonies. That is why it put the main emphasis on the development of naval power, which was a necessary instrument in its strategy to prevail in the global economic and military power game. British naval programmes were predicated on the usefulness of battleships which were considered "symbols of the British victory at Trafalgar" (Kaldor 1981, p. 34).

The British share of global sea power was about one-half throughout the nineteenth century, but it started to decline from the late 1890s onwards. Despite rapid absolute growth of its naval expenditures, Britain was not able to retain its quantitative and qualitative edge unharmed in comparison to its main challengers (Modelski and Thompson 1987, pp. 121-3, 202-10). In particular the rise of the German navy had a major impact on British military strategy and economy.

In Anglo-German relations commercial and power-political rivalries could not be disentangled from each other. The German economic challenge was interpreted in Britain, because of its simultaneous naval expansion, as a geopolitical challenge as well (Kennedy 1982, pp. 313-20).   Britain as the declining power had to face a simultaneous economic and strategic challenge from Germany, while the United States, being located overseas, was competing only in the economic arena. This was due to the British decision to co-operate voluntarily with the United States in the transfer of political and military predominance to it.

In contrast to its global naval expansion, the military commitment of Britain to the European continent was relatively weak, even though it existed politically. "The General Staff had embraced the continental commitment without having the means at their disposal to carry it out" (French 1982, p. 27).   The British policy of non-commitment was made feasible by a balance of power based until the 1890s, and to a lesser extent since then, on an intricate system of military alliances on the European continent. In this context, "the managed balance of power can be seen as a kind of subsidy for the British imperial expansion in the nineteenth century" (Mandelbaum 1988, p. 36). Without this opportunity to abstain from the "continental commitment" Britain would hardly have had chances to maintain its dominant global position. That position was both reflected and facilitated by the priority given to the navy over the army.

The political structure of Europe permitted Britain to keep its army small. This policy was supported by the domestic economic and political aversion to a standing army, which was regarded as a drain on industrial development and a potential threat to the liberal political system. The expansion of the army would also have increased the level of taxation which was considered politically unacceptable. The Smithian orthodoxy, while admitting the need for national defence against external threats, considered the army unproductive and thus unnecessary during times of peace. In effect, the British nineteenth century attitude towards the military, until the shock created by the Boer War, can be characterized as public apathy (Johnson 1960, p. 13, 40; French 1982, pp. 8-9; Porter 1983, pp. 18-20).

The relatively small size of the British army can be explained by its virtual absence from the European continent, which made it possible to devote it to colonial missions. They were directed primarily against local uprisings and were thus carried out by limited on-site forces and expeditionary troops despatched from the home island. The asymmetries in the military situation of the colonies and the lack of "equal enemies" neither provided the army with relevant organizational knowledge, nor prepared it for the consequences of modern technology. As a result, the British army relied on the primacy of the offensive, even though new technologies had already altered the strategic logic of war (Spiers 1980, pp. 206-10, 230; Robbins 1983, pp. 37-8).

New strategic pressures surfaced, however, to increase the size of the British army and to restructure it. Improved overland communications, made possible by the proliferation of railways, facilitated more effective military operations by adversaries, especially Russia, against various parts of the empire (Friedberg 1988, pp. 273-4). At the turn of the century fears of a German invasion of the British Isles, though largely unfounded, started to influence domestic political and military opinion in favour of a bigger army. This gave rise to a competition between the "blue water" and "big army" schools, but hardly resulted in a systematic strategic development of the military forces (Johnson 1960, pp. 37-9).

For instance, no clear-cut preference was accorded to either European or colonial missions for the army. However, the overall result was the relative strengthening of the army. It expanded quite vigorously during the Boer War and again in 1912-13. In 1910 the share of the military personnel of the British male population aged 20-44 was 4.5 per cent, but it jumped to 6.4 per cent in 1913. At that time it reached the same relative level as German military manpower (Flora 1983, p. 249, p. 252).

In the beginning, British air power was conceived and developed primarily for colonial missions. Aircraft provided a rapid and effective means of access to the far-flung parts of the British empire. In that way new technology was used to cement imperial unity. The use of aircraft in various colonial wars in the early 1910s also proved that they could be utilized effectively in difficult conditions (Paris 1989).

The army reform had been debated after the Boer War, and was partially implemented by the Haldane reforms. They started to reorient the military structure and planning of the army towards the continental strategy that stressed the ability for the rapid mobilization and equipment of forces. The gradual switch to continental missions took place, however, under growing economic constraints, as the economic resources decreased in relative terms and public spending for social purposes had also to be expanded (Spiers 1980, pp. 266-70; French 1982, pp. 14-15). The Haldane reforms were only partial and the underlying problems of the army surfaced again in 1914. In the first months of World War I, the deficiencies in manpower, weaponry and tactics forced the British government to redefine its army policy, under the leadership of Field Marshall Kitchener, in order to adjust it to the conditions of warfare in Europe (Simkins 1981).

While the development of the army before World War I started from a rather modest level, the British navy had already been for decades a formidable force in control of the sea lanes. The development of the navy was influenced by the Mahanian thinking on the nature of sea power. This thinking emphasized the construction of battleships and their concentrated use in naval operations (Friedberg 1988, pp. 139-44). A characteristic of the battleship is that it requires constant technical improvements in its mobility, survivability, and firepower against other comparable forces.

The rise of political tensions and the action-reaction process in armament dynamics fuelled and justified the Anglo-German technological arms race before World War I. Such races are expensive, since improved quality usually costs more than the increased quantity. That is why the Anglo-German naval race drove up military expenditure and reduced the number of ships that could be constructed. The cost escalation resulted in bottlenecks in the construction programmes and exacerbated domestic conflicts between the opponents and proponents of the naval programmes (Berghahn 1971).

The preference for battleships is typical of a dominant naval power, which likes to compare its fighting capacity directly with that of other powers. The British two-power standard, with all its ambiguities, is a good example of the tendency, in peacetime comparisons, to confront rival battlefleets head-on. The dominant power, once it has attained a lead in critical military technologies, usually tries to freeze their development in order to perpetuate its advantage (Wainstein 1971, p. 163). This proved to be impossible, however, in the Anglo-German naval race, partly because of domestic opposition; interest groups supporting naval rearmament were well organized both in Britain and in Germany (Kennedy 1982, pp. 369-74). In addition, technological innovation, a critical ingredient in every new round of the arms spiral, became institutionalized in British and German industries (McNeill 1982, pp. 277-81).

As World War I approached, the British military establishment and strategy faced entirely new requirements for which it was ill-prepared. Britain became "a victim both of geography and of changing technology" (Kennedy 1981, pp. 181-6). Already before the war the British military outlays had, in relative terms, been somewhat higher than in other industrialized countries. This was due, in the first place, to the need to maintain "not a single but two military and naval establishments; one for domestic defence and another for protection of the Empire" (Davis and Huttenback 1988, p. 133).

The costs of defending the British Isles were about the same as the total military expenditures of Germany and France each. The expenses of the colonial military and naval establishment, though somewhat smaller than the costs of defending the home island, added a substantial sum to the British military outlays. The high price of the military defence of the dominions and colonies, which themselves paid only a small portion of the expenses, was justified by the need to protect not only shipping and foreign trade, but also the export of capital and financial services. In reality, the military umbrella opened above the empire, and the empire itself was a major factor in pushing Britain towards a relative decline (Davis and Huttenback 1988, pp. 129-36; O'Brien 1990, pp. 37-40).

The intensification of military and political competition between major powers increased the spending requirements. In Britain the economic resources had to be mobilized from an economy whose relative strength was declining, but in which the level of costs was still high. From the late nineteenth century onwards both military expenditure and military production started to increase and their real cost, which had been high before, became even higher (O'Brien 1990, pp. 36-7, 42).

To assuage the military appetite the British government, following the liberal model, allocated the military contracts mainly to private manufacturers of weapons, such as Armstrong, Vickers and Yarrow (Kaldor 1981, pp. 31-4). The preference given to private companies created serious problems when Britain mobilized during the Boer War, and even more so during World War I. As the British army was prepared essentially for small colonial wars, the armaments industry was not prepared for a lengthy war with other industrial powers (Kennedy 1987, p. 229). There was also a manpower problem, as both industry and the military services, especially the army, chased the labour force for their specific needs (Johnson 1960, pp. 136-8).

In the absence of consistent governmental policy, the private companies had not built up sufficient reserves of guns and shells; and even if they had the equipment such as artillery was not necessarily fit for trench warfare. This joint failure of public policy and the armaments industry affected the army more seriously than the navy, which traditionally had had close relations with the industry. In order to be available in war, capital-intensive battleships have to be constructed before the war, while the army can, in theory, be replenished more quickly. World War I, however, was different from what was expected, and, as a land war, put a heavy demand upon industrial capacity and manpower (Trebilcock 1975; French 1982, pp. 39-45).

The British problems of industrial mobilization in World War I were due largely to Britain's commitment to maintain global naval superiority in order to counter the German challenge and to arrest the decline of its international position. The price of this commitment was the inadequate preparedness of the arms industry for a general war. The decision of the British government to stick to a small, albeit expanding army had a direct bearing on the arms industry. In munitions production for the army, private companies did not receive governmental contracts and, for this reason, turned to the international market in which they became very active (French 1982, pp. 47-8).

In naval weaponry the British story is different; the new generation of technically educated officers concluded close ties with the private arms manufacturers. The public allocation of military contracts to private companies was initially justified, among other things, by the need to create employment in the conditions of depression which plagued the British economy in the mid-1880s. Arms contracts were intended to strengthen the economy and Britain's international position as well (McNeill 1982, pp. 268-71, 273-4).

Britain's International Position

As suggested above, the international economic position of Britain may account better for the fluctuations in the military spending and industrial capacity than the long-cycle theories. In this context, the economic wealth of Britain is pivotal for the understanding of its grand strategy: "Britain could play its full part in defeating Germany by relying on the Royal Navy to protect its own economy and on its allies to fight the land war whilst the British provided them with all the munitions and supplies they required" (French 1982, p. 35). By keeping its economy strong and going during the war, Britain could not only continue commanding the seas, but could also subsidize the allies fighting the land war in Europe on its behalf.

In this argument, the critical issue is whether the British economy, despite its relative decline, was strong enough to shoulder the dual military burden on the seas and on the European continent. The response to this query must take into account both short-term and long-term considerations. Even if Britain was able to finance the military missions for a relatively brief period of time, the expanding military spending could, over the long term, undermine its international position and distort the domestic economic structure. In this case the political and military success of the national security strategy was bought at the expense of continuing and perhaps even accelerating economic decline.

It seems to be an established fact that in spite of the absolute growth in Britain's military spending its relative burden remained so limited that there was prior to 1913 no significant trade-off between military allocations on the one hand and capital investments and economic growth on the other. Thus, the hypothesis that such a trade-off is particularly acute in a declining hegemon does not receive consistent support (Rasler and Thompson 1988, pp. 76-7). That is why the causes of British economic dilemmas must be sought from other sources, which may not, however, be entirely separate from military expenditure and production.

The economic faculty of Britain to compete with other core powers decreased significantly in the decades preceding World War I. It is often claimed that extensive overseas investments retarded industrial growth within Britain. This point has been argued in different ways; for instance, by suggesting that capital investments abroad went to primary sectors of economy and thus favoured the established industries at home that needed raw materials. Instead of contributing to technological and institutional innovation in the British economy foreign investments reinforced its structural rigidities (Kirby 1981, pp. 14-16).

By creating new demand, British capital exports contributed to the expansion of international trade and helped to maintain free trade (Mathias 1983, p. 302). On average, about one-third of British savings went abroad between 1870 and 1914, and during the peak periods of foreign investments, as in 1886-90 and 1906-14, the outflows surpassed domestic investments. This may have undermined the strategic sectors of the British economy, including chemicals, electrical engineering and motor cars, in which no significant export capacity was developed (Mathias 1983, pp. 298, 303). These trends were reinforced by the flow of British exports to primary producing countries, which did not challenge the economy to technological and institutional innovation.

On the other hand, the crowding-out effect of foreign investments has been put in doubt by several other studies. They observe that even though the development of domestic industry may have occasionally suffered from foreign investments, they did not significantly harm it. Instead, the relative economic decline of Britain was obviously more due to self-generated domestic factors. They included the failure of entrepreneurship, an inimical attitude among the ruling class towards modern technical education, and the obstacles raised by the trade unions to technological innovations, which all weakened the country's ability to keep up on the development of new technologies (Landes 1981, pp. 350-2; Matthews, Feinstein and Odling-Smee 1982, pp. 353-7; Pollard 1989, pp. 99-100; Mokyr 1990, pp. 261-6).

High prices for industrial products were enough to satisfy the British exporters, and made them oblivious of product improvements and market shares. Meanwhile, the exporters of the rising powers, protected by tariff walls, pushed their products forward in the new strategic industrial sectors. This helped them to conquer an increasing share of the British market and make it more dependent on the international economic environment (Kirby 1981, pp. 20-1). Britain was thus forced increasingly to resort to its empire as the outlet for export products, and its political and military functions were capital-inflated.

The economic consequences of the empire for Britain should not be exaggerated, however. It obviously called for military resources, but it did not require, after all, that much in the way of capital funds. British capital exports increased from an annual average of £40 million in 1865-74 through £98 million in 1885-94 to £173 million in 1905-14. The bulk of these funds went, however, to North America and South America and the empire absorbed only between one-fourth and one-fifth of the total (Davis and Huttenback 1988, pp. 35-44).

Military Production and Spin-offs

The foregoing analysis shows that the most crucial failure in the British economy was the inability to move to the new industrial sectors and technologies that its rivals occupied. This economic failure had direct military repercussions. There was a lack of "more active efforts to preserve and develop Britain's defence industrial base. Steel and shipbuilding were allowed to deteriorate, chemical and electromechanical devices lagged far behind" (Friedberg 1988, p. 296). This development posed a clear and present danger to the political and military position of Britain in the world that had depended on the size and technological advance of its navy. The naval expansion of other powers and the construction of railways across the European and Asian continents weakened Britain's maritime supremacy and, in consequence, its world leadership. As Britain drew the necessary conclusions from this development and started withdrawing its naval forces to European waters to counter Germany, the dissolution of its empire was accelerated (Friedberg 1988, pp. 298-300).

Research results concerning the relative economic decline of Britain are, at best, conflicting. Its external economic relations appear to have contributed to its decline by reducing incentives more than resources to invest in the renewal of civilian industries at home. This weakened the material basis of Britain, while the economic and military competition with Germany absorbed, at the same time, increasing amounts of most advanced domestic resources. There seems to have been a downward spiral in which the absolute and relative growth of the military burden and economic decline reinforced each other through a variety of intermediary mechanisms.

Even more important, however, was the domestic failure to eliminate structural defects in the economy and to inject new dynamism into it. In other words, the British decline was self-generated. For instance, in the iron and steel industry the entrepreneurial failures, due to its familial control, appear to have been the single most important source of problems (Payne 1968, pp. 94-6). Similarly, in the electrical industry the British loss to Germany and the United States has been traced to the small size of the enterprises and the fragmented character of the industry in Britain. Such an industrial structure was not able to launch the large-scale R&D projects that would have been necessary to maintain the British edge in the fierce technological competition within the international market at the turn of the century (Hall and Preston 1988, pp. 110-122).

The military factor is relevant in both the external and internal explanation of the British decline. In the external explanation the growing military burden is considered a factor which reinforced and even accelerated the economic decline, but did not cause it. In that regard, however, one should avoid too easy and mechanical answers to complex problems. That is why it is useful to explore the alternative hypothesis that investments in military R&D not only increased the technological sophistication of weapons, but also spilled over to the civilian sector. As the relative economic decline persisted, however, these spin-off effects were not obviously strong enough to cancel out various adverse effects and, in the internal explanation, to rectify domestic failures.

The spin-off argument presupposes, of course, that military technology was advancing. This was no doubt the case, as the pre-World War I arms race was genuinely technological in character. The development costs of weapons systems were high and often unpredictable, but the resources so invested also yielded results: "military technology came to constitute the leading edge of British and (world) engineering and technical development . . . Overall, it seems clear that as arms firms became pioneers of one new technology after another . . . they evolved quickly into vast bureaucratic structures of a quasi-public character " (McNeill 1982, pp. 285, 292). The increasing technological sophistication of weapons systems was built in the strategic competition between Britain and Germany, and had implications for military strategy and tactics (Pearton 1982, pp. 117-31).

The development of military technology before World War I has been assumed to have had a beneficial impact on the civilian economy of Britain. Clive Trebilcock, in particular, has claimed that "armament research and armament technology played a leading role in developing the most advanced civilian technologies to be found in Britain between 1890 and 1914" (Trebilcock 1976, p. 97). His argument states that after having been a technical laggard for decades, the British arms industry embarked in the late 1870s on a rapid trajectory of development which yielded new, technically advanced weapons for the army, navy and air force (Trebilcock 1969, pp. 479-81).

The British arms manufacturers innovated both in materials, such as special steels, and in production methods. In the United States the industrial system was transformed by the introduction, first, of machine tools and then the mass-production of components and interchangeable parts which were assembled into complex products. In the United States the "American system of manufacture" started from the arms industry of the north-east and spread over to the production of typewriters, sewing machines and watches. Both the civilian and military sectors of the British industry were far behind in the adoption of new techniques and organization of production (Clapham 1951, pp. 152-6; Trebilcock 1969, pp. 483-4; Pollard 1989, pp. 19-20).

The production of arms with interchangeable parts started in Britain only in the 1850s and the 1860s - that is, decades later than in the United States - and even then the scale of production was modest (Landes 1981, p. 308). Later on, in particular from the 1880s onwards, the situation may have changed, however. The new precise production techniques permitted the arms firms to expand to bicycles and motor cars, and in that way they were able also to diversify their production lines (Trebilcock 1969, pp. 486-7). Yet doubts remain, for the evidence of the military origins of industrial production relying on machine tools is scanty at best (Landes 1981, pp. 308-15).

The British industry experienced an extensive amalgamation movement around the turn of the century and new companies were attached to the production chain. In that way vertical integration and combination became a practice, for example, in the shipbuilding industry. This development may have eroded the ability of the industry to develop and produce new types of ships (Pollard 1989, pp. 24-5). Armstrong, Vickers and other arms manufacturers developed vertical integration from steel production through armour-making to the construction of battleships and tanks. This was achieved usually by acquiring small firms in supporting industries. As a result, the great armament companies were surrounded by subsidiary firms producing components, guns and ammunition for major weapons systems. The pressure to integrate vertically was weaker in the iron and steel firms catering for the civilian market (Clapham 1951, pp. 260-2, 269-70).

In a sense, the dependence of arms manufacturers on public authorities and their tendency to build autonomous lines of production were complementary, but at the same time this isolated them from the competitive pressures of the market. In order to keep the equipment and capital in continual use the arms manufacturers had to achieve a sufficient volume of production which the British navy, and even less the army, could not assure. This called for the export of arms. The capacity to export existed, as the arms firms were large, sometimes clumsy, conglomerates which had access to financial and technological resources. And export they did: British arms manufacturers controlled 60 per cent of the international weapons market in 1900-14 (Kaldor 1981, p. 37; McNeill 1982, pp. 271-2).

The development of military technology probably benefited, in a limited manner, the civilian industry, while its international dissemination certainly eroded Britain's economic position in the world. British arms manufacturers established weapons factories and arsenals in economically less-developed countries, such as Russia, Spain and Turkey. In these countries arms manufacturing not only brought in new technical knowledge and economic institutions, but also encouraged capital-goods industries in general. Arms production demonstrated how modern industries work and created new demand for educated manpower, new materials and productive industrial organization. In that way, the spread of the British arms industry, especially naval production, created a positive spin-off process in the receiving country (Trebilcock 1976, p. 98-100).

Taking all the threads together, the remaining puzzle is: how can the alleged technical and organizational progress of the arms manufacturers be reconciled with the undisputable decline of the British industry and economy in general? To my mind, the answer has to be found in the structural condition of the British industry. Its leading industrial sectors matured and gradually lost their competitive capacity. Instead of investing significantly in new industries with a higher growth potential Britain concentrated on those industries "which had enabled her to achieve an early lead, but which now had reached the end of their growth potential, and/or which newly industrializing countries could set up most easily in competition". A complementary reason for the British decline was the reluctance of its industry to "adopt radically new methods, particularly those requiring high-level science and technology, and new forms of internal organization". The British economy was stuck in the traditional, slow-growth path of development from which it became increasingly difficult to switch to the high-growth path at the technical edge (Pollard 1989, pp. 55-7; see also Landes 1981, pp. 234-7).

The international economic competition intensified steadily at the turn of the nineteenth century. This was very visible, for instance, in the steel industry, in which Britain lost ground to Germany and the United States. As the vulnerability of British iron and steel producers to international competition increased they made efforts to shield themselves from its adverse effects. The manufacturing sector was divided in its attitude towards the tariff movement. Its supporters included the industries most heavily exposed to international competition such as iron and steel as well as the chemical industry. On the other hand, most finished manufacturers were in favour of lower tariffs. (Gourevitch 1986, pp. 77-81; Pollard 1989, pp. 239-40).

Another manifestation of the effort to seek shelter from competition was the decision of major corporations, such as Armstrong and Vickers, to move increasingly into armaments production. In so doing they became closely linked with the Admiralty, developed their own bureaucratic structures and insulated themselves from the foreign competition. In effect, Armstrong and Vickers ceased to deal with the Admiralty on a market basis and developed a quasi-public framework for their collaboration with the authorities. This permitted them to divide between them first the British and then the international arms market. (McNeill 1982, pp. 289-91). The safeguarded position of arms manufacturers tended to make them resistant to technical innovations; for instance, Armstrong and Vickers were totally uninterested in exploiting the benefits of the diesel engine (Saul 1968, p. 218).

The rigidity of the institutional structure of the British economy, particularly in the shipbuilding and steel industries, decelerated the pace of innovations and limited them to product improvements. In general, the British failed in research and development; industrial research was deficient and did not produce enough good innovations (Hall and Preston 1988, pp. 116-21). The availability of public funds through military spending permitted the leading companies in shipbuilding and steelmaking to continue the narrow and impotent policy of innovation. Thus they shunned the structural adjustments which would have been necessary to switch the economy into the next, technically more advanced, high-growth gear.

The slowness of restructuring in military-related industries made the reliance on armament contracts even greater. In that way military spending "channelled innovation and investment further into a technological cul-de-sac, preserving and perfecting an outmoded nineteenth-century industrial structure and denying the emergence of more modern markets and methods of manufacture" (Kaldor 1981, pp. 39-42). Ultimately, the anomalies in the political structure and decision-making of Britain, and the consequent inability to develop effective public strategies for industrial renewal, perpetuated the structural dilemma of its economy (Pollard 1989, pp. 258-9).

These anomalies were associated with the increasing prevalence of conservative, anti-industrial values in Britain. From the late nineteenth century onwards, the criticism of the material greed and social disruption, associated by intellectuals and policy-makers alike with the industrial revolution, created anti-urban and anti-industrial attitudes which were hardly conducive to economic growth. In reality, "the social and intellectual revolution implicit in industrialism was muted, perhaps even aborted. Instead, a compromise was effected, accommodating new groups, new interests, and new needs within a social and cultural matrix that preserved the forms and even many of the values of tradition" (Wiener 1981, pp. 81-90, 157-9). Related criticism was expressed much earlier by Thorstein Veblen who pointedly explored the British predilection for conspicuous consumption. In particular, in comparison to the Germans the British were lacking industrial efficiency and devoted their time to fashion, leisure sports and other unnecessary concerns (Veblen 1915, pp. 134-44).

In the British thinking, the industrial way of life was associated with the United States rather than with Britain. The expansion and innovation in the industrial production did not stop, however, and there were positive spin-offs from the military to the civilian industries (Kaldor 1981, pp. 40-1). They occurred, however, mostly in the light and medium industries such as the production of rifles, sewing machines, bicycles and other vehicles (Trebilcock 1969, pp. 485-7). They did not reach out to the crucial capital-goods industries where international competition was heavy and gains big, and where civilian and military needs coexisted. The spin-off potential becomes much smaller when the interrelated military and civilian technologies are specialized and have developed their own technological trajectories (Trebilcock 1976, pp. 103-4).

The spin-offs in naval construction were smaller than in other industries. Naval investments also had significant opportunity costs, as they particularly diverted public funds away from alternative civilian uses. In other words, naval construction absorbed considerable amounts of productive resources without really contributing, through innovation spin-offs, to the industrial renewal of Britain. Before World War I the expenditures of the British navy expanded and climbed, for instance, in 1903-4 to about £40 million. This represented more than a quarter of total public expenditure (Friedberg 1988, p. 131). In 1909 the McKenna programme was adopted that supported the building of eight Dreadnoughts immediately and ten more over the next two years.

This did not suffice, however: in addition to its economic leadership Britain also lost its naval supremacy; other naval powers also innovated during this period of rapid technical change (Robbins 1983, p. 38).

The verdict in the British case appears to be that the military spending did not, in and of itself, cause its economic decline. For long periods the relative military burdens were rather low and could not engender extensive economic effects. Furthermore, the relative decline started at least two decades before the adversity with Germany had developed into a serious political and military rivalry and had started to absorb extensive economic resources. Once this happened, however, Britain was already weakened by the decline and the increasing expenditure for military purposes before and during World War I damaged the productivity and growth prospects of its economy (Rosecrance 1990, pp. 59-60).

The primary cause of the British decline is a combination of external and internal factors, among which domestic failures and inabilities dominate. They were reinforced by the institutional structures created by the expanding arms industries, and blocked the needed innovations in new capital-goods sectors. Spin-offs from the military to civilian industries took place. They were confined, however, to light and medium industries and were not strong enough to cancel out the lack of innovation and restructuring in capital-goods industries in which military production had, in fact, adverse effects.

Chapter 4
Military Production and the US Decline

Is the United States Declining?

The United States of the post-World War II era has been often compared with Great Britain of the pre-World War I period. They were both international economic hegemonies and political system leaders. Both maintained extensive military establishments, in particular, navies, and large arms industries to prop up their system-wide leadership and to make their international commitments credible.

Global leadership is costly, however, because of the decreasing returns and increasing costs of protection and political dominance (Gilpin 1981, pp. 168-75). Basically, these costs are produced by imperial overextension and overspending which tends to reinforce the vicious circle of economic decline. "If a state overextends itself strategically . . . it runs the risk that the potential benefits from external expansion may be outweighed by the great expense of it all" (Kennedy 1987, p. xvi). This conclusion is supported by evidence, but forgets about the importance of the context; the nature and impact of the imperial overextension obviously depends on the global configuration of economic and military power.

There are different views on whether it is justified to establish an analogy between the British pre-World War I decline and the US post-World War II experience. The world-system approach has, in particular, inclined to compare the domestic economic dynamics and the international economic context of Britain's decline with that of the United States. In practical terms, this means that the relative decline of Britain in 1873-96 has been compared with the US decline after 1967 in terms of the following factors: loss of productive superiority, passing of organizational advantage, high mass standard of living, underinvestment in research and development, and persistence of free trade policies (Goldfrank 1983).

On the other hand, the analogy between the British and US declines has been denied by several authors. Joseph S. Nye stresses the special factors in the experiences of both countries. In effect, Nye finds four major differences between the two hegemonic powers: the degree of predominance, the economies of scale, the choice of types and levels of military commitments, and geopolitical challenges (Nye 1990, pp. 63-7).

In Nye's view, the United States does not face now any power political challenge comparable with the German pressure before World War I which overstretched Britain more seriously than the burdens of the empire (Nye 1990, pp. 57-8). A similar point is made by John A. Hall who observes that the US position is less challenged because "its geopolitical rival stands outside capitalist society, whilst its capitalist economic rivals are geopolitically dependent on it". In addition, the Soviet Union is rapidly declining, while the imperial Germany as a challenger of Britain was a rising power (Hall 1990, pp. 135-7).

On the other hand, both the absolute and relative economic burden of military leadership is higher now than during the era of British hegemony. Such a cost explosion - due to the need for expensive and complex advanced technologies - affects, however, all the military powers, not only the United States. Some of them, especially the Soviet Union, are even worse equipped than the United States to shoulder the military burden on their economic development (Gill 1990, p. 82).

In a historical perspective, the United States may have been saved so far because its overall economic position has been stronger and more broadly based than the British position before World War I. That is why it has been able to muddle through the economic burden of a relatively high level of military spending. This is reflected in the fact that there are no powers seriously contesting the US political and military primacy. This leads to the situation that even though the United States is facing increasingly tough economic competition, mainly from its own military-political allies, "there is no combined military and economic challenger". From this it is concluded that the "costs of international leadership have greatly declined" (Rosecrance 1990, pp. 61-2; cf. Nye 1990, pp. 111-70). A somewhat different conclusion would be that the US economic strength has helped it to survive in competition with other major powers since they, also investing heavily in military spending, have to carry a greater relative burden. The United States is constantly losing out, however, to those powers which are oriented to the commercial market rather than to the military power.

The critical issue in the debate is, of course, whether the United States is in relative decline or not. Ample criticism has been put forward against the view that the US economy is on the decline and that, as a consequence, international economic and political stability is in jeopardy. The basic empirical argument against the declinist thesis is that statistical evidence on the relative economic decline of the United States is meagre and contradictory. It might also be pointed out that the yardsticks of evaluation have been inadequate and even misleading. Instead of the US national share of global production, a more valid measure would be the share of world GNP controlled by US companies (Hall 1990, pp. 132-5).

At the conceptual level it is emphasized that the nature of power in international relations has so changed that the cross-national comparisons of power distributions over time do not reveal the real state of affairs. Power is more structural than behavioural, it is more based on consent than on coercion, and is more intangible than measurable. It is suggested that the United States is still able to use effective structural and cultural domination and exercise power over outcomes of political and economic processes in interdependent international relations. That is why the declinist thesis is empirically and, even more so, conceptually misleading (Russett 1985; Strange 1987; Nye 1990, pp. 173-201; Gill 1990, pp. 63-4).

The continued military primacy of the the United States means that it is spending, both in absolute and relative terms, much more for military purposes in general and for R&D in particular than its main economic competitors (for statistics, see Thee 1990, pp. 13-16) . Obviously, the difference in the military burdens of Great Britain and its main economic challengers was smaller at the turn of the century than it has been in the post-World War II period between the United States and its rivals (Kennedy 1987, pp. 531-2). This disparity in the British and US experiences apparently implies that the relative impact of military spending on the domestic economies of the major powers has been different in these two historical contexts. In comparison to its economic rivals the relative burden was higher in Britain.

There is no agreement among the scholars on whether, and especially how, US relative power in international relations has in reality declined. It appears that its share of world trade and production has decreased from the late 1940s to the present. The US share of the total world output fell from 45 per cent in the late 1940s to 25 per cent in the mid-1960s, but has remained relatively constant since then (Friedberg 1989, pp. 402-3). Other authors suggest that the decline, measured by the US share of the total world product, continued until the early 1970s, but has been arrested since then (Nye 1990, pp. 73-6).

The relative decline of the United States seems to have stopped in the 1960s if its share of the total world industrial output is used as the yardstick, but only in the 1970s if it is related to the economic capability of the OECD area. The relative decline may have stopped even later if the percentage of US exports of the total OECD exports is used as the criterion (Nau 1990, pp. 63-5). Nau's analysis shows that the stabilization of the US economic position within the industrial world is of a more recent origin than in the world economy as a whole. The stabilization may be explained by the global economic crisis of the 1970s when the difference between the United States and its main competitors narrowed in comparison to the growth years.

The political debate in the United States has been worried about the deindustrialization of its economy, due to the switch to a service economy. This change has, plausibly enough, been assumed to have adverse effects on the national military capability since it has jeopardized the technological superiority on which the United States has relied in its military strategy (Seabury 1983; Defense Technology Base 1988, pp. 2-3). The deindustrialization thesis has been contested, however, by pointing out that the share of manufacturing of the GNP has remained constant throughout the post-World War II period, even though there have been changes in the composition of the manufacturing output (Friedberg 1989, pp. 405-6).

The deindustrialization of an economy and the slow growth of its productivity have sometimes been equated with each other. In a developed economy this is not necessarily the case, however. If there is an identifiable shift from manufacturing to services, the productivity per input in industry may be growing and the labour force so released moves to services where productivity is generally lower. In other words, a decline in overall productivity does not necessarily mean that the competitiveness of a nation's industry is eroding. The industry may become leaner, but at the same time meaner.

In the United States the growth rate of productivity has fluctuated widely since World War II, but the trend line has pointed upwards. In fact, the United States still has, in spite of the decelerated growth rate, the highest absolute level of manufacturing productivity in the world. However, it has been growing more rapidly in other industrial countries, in particular, in Japan, Italy, France and West Germany. That is why a kind of convergence effect has operated to even out the US advantage (Pianta 1988, pp. 27-30; Baumol 1989, pp. 611-15). It is significant that all those countries whose manufacturing productivity is approaching the US level are its most serious economic competitors.

The reasons for the declining growth rates in manufacturing productivity in the United States are manifold, including the impact of the 1973 oil crisis and the shifts to lower productivity sectors. Empirical studies give rather mixed results regarding the relative impact of various factors on production because of the differences in data, indicators and time periods (Wolff 1985). It has not been shown conclusively that military spending *per se* would undermine a nation's productivity to any significant degree (Gold 1991, p. 43). However, military spending may have indirect effects on productivity and its rate of growth, and there seems to be a negative macro-economic correlation between the share of GNP devoted to the military and the rate of productivity growth.

One of the potential explanations of the slowdown in the productivity growth is the scarcity of commercially viable inventions available to the industry. Military-related research has, it is true, produced a considerable number of inventions which have been utitilized in the commercial civilian market as well. Yet the the US economy, because of its sheer size, would have needed more of such inventions. The extensive allocation of R&D funds for military purposes has deprived the civilian industry of the innovative resources it would have badly needed. The spin-off effect from the military R&D to the civilian applications has worked, but not efficiently enough. Marketable products can be best created by applying R&D funds directly for their development instead of expecting the military research to do the job indirectly.

A basic issue here is that the bulk of military R&D is devoted to specific technological applications, while only a small part of it goes to basic research. By strengthening the innovative infrastructure of the economy, basic research is an important source of renewal and, more importantly, innovations which can be converted into marketable products. By absorbing human and financial resources from basic research, military R&D erodes the basis of productivity growth. Its performance would have been improved by allocating resources, say, to the development of flexible production technologies, such as CADCAM systems, instead of improving manoeuvrability and undetectability of fighter aircraft (deGrasse 1983, pp. 104-6; Markusen 1986, pp. 503-5; Lucas 1990, pp. 93-4).

Since the 1960s the US civilian and military technologies have been spreading - thanks to the global reach of its transnational corporations - to the hands of its competitors. There has not been comparable reverse flow of technological knowledge back to the United States that would have balanced the situation. On the contrary, the US share in the world exports of high-tech product groups has decreased and their trade balances are turning into the red; their imports have been growing in the 1980s much more rapidly than their exports (Gilpin 1981, pp. 175-85; Friedberg 1989, pp.

423-6; Gill 1990, pp. 67-9). In fact, the British experience before World War II is comparable in that regard.

Military R&D

Extensive allocation of human R&D resources to military purposes in the United States - the estimates vary between 15 and 35 per cent of engineers and scientists - has made a dent in the potential progress of civilian technology and productivity growth (Dumas 1982, pp. 11-21; deGrasse 1983, pp. 101-2). In addition, a minimum of one-half of the federal R&D funds have been directed to military purposes. During the Reagan years, this share approached three-quarters, especially in such cutting-edge technologies as lasers, artificial intelligence and new materials (Stowsky 1986, pp. 697-9). To get a longer view, one can observe that in 1980 the military R&D absorbed 47 per cent of the total US federal spending on R&D, while in 1990 the corresponding figure was 61 per cent (Carey 1991, p. 99).

The real value of US military R&D spending, in the 1988 prices, decreased from some $30 billion in the early 1960s to little over $20 billion in the mid-1970s. Then, the absolute military R&D figures of the United States had converged to the level of the total R&D expenditure of Japan. Since then the US military R&D and the total Japanese R&D have grown hand in hand, both reaching the level of $40 billion in 1987-88 (Ramses 90, p. 234).

This example hints at the pivotal importance of the military R&D for the overall technological and economic development of the United States. This point is underpinned by the fact that from the late 1960s to the late 1970s the civilian R&D in the United States remained static. This was reflected in the reduced propensity of private US firms to put money into basic research and risky long-term projects (Mansfield 1980, pp. 572-3; Hills 1983, pp. 207-9). In general, the "result has been a reduced pace of innovation in the US economy, while the technological competition from Europe and Japan has been increasing" (Pianta 1988, p. 132).

The United States invested proportionally less and less money for civilian R&D, which was, in turn, expanding rapidly in Europe and, in particular, in Japan. There the military R&D has absorbed in 1987 only 5 per cent of the total R&D funds, while the corresponding US share was more than ten-fold (Thee 1990, p. 13) . Obviously, in order to be able to compete with Japanese companies, the United States should have developed an effective "covert" industrial policy based on the resources spent for the military R&D, so as to sponsor in that way the technological dynamism of firms in the international commercial market.

In evaluating the impact of military R&D one can observe that in the United States risk minimization and routine product engineering by large teams of scholars and engineers, rather than focusing on new process innovations, have been hallmarks in the development of military technology. The emphasis has been on technologies that fit the existing military missions and are accepted by the military bureaucracies, who often resist advanced technologies requiring new military strategies and institutional structures (Gansler 1989, pp. 217-8).

These priorities tend to distort the industry structures by increasing their inefficiency and rigidity. Thus, there is little incentive to increase productivity either in the military industry or, as a result, in the entire economy (Gansler 1980, pp. 99-108; Reppy 1985, pp. 13-14; Stein 1985, pp. 346-7). In fact, a coherent industrial policy should create a variety of incentives, in contrast to administrative directives, to increase productivity in the manufacture of military goods (Gansler 1987, pp. 57-8).

As observed earlier, the shortcomings in the industrial structure and productivity should be reflected in the nation's relative position in the international trade of high-technology products. It is a more sophisticated measure of the relative economic standing than the share of total industrial production alone. In practically all the fields of advanced technology in which military interests dominate, the U.S. companies have lost civilian market share, primarily to their Japanese competitors. This applies, among others, to such research- and technology-intensive fields as electronics, robotics, machine tools and semiconductors (deGrasse 1983, pp. 102-4). From 1976 to 1983 the United States enjoyed an annual surplus of some $20 billion in the high-tech trade, but in 1984-88 the average surplus was reduced to about $3-4 billion (Ramses 1989, p. 236). The balance has gone into the red especially with Japan and the newly-industrializing economies (NIEs) of Asia, while in 1987 exports of high-tech products to other countries exceeded their imports by only about $30 million (Chesnais 1990, p. 8).

These trends hold even if one takes a longer time perspective; the US share of world high-tech exports has decreased somewhat from the 1960s to the 1980s, while import penetration into the US market by the other exporters has grown markedly. However, the share of advanced technologies of US imports is lower, 24 per cent, than of its exports, 40 per cent. In other words, the United States has lost its dominance in the manufacture and sale of high-tech products, while its exports have remained dependent on them. On the other hand, Japan's relative standing has improved (Shinohara 1991, pp. 14-16) . Yet, despite the global proliferation of the United States technological capabilities and the consequences for its trade balances in high-tech products, it is still clearly the leading industrial power in the world economy (Friedberg 1989, pp. 406-8; Chesnais 1990, p. 8; Nye 1990, p. 77).

Military Roots of the Economic Decline

In principle, there are two different views on the importance of the military industry for the US economy. In the first alternative it has been considered a Schumpeterian leading sector which has had a pervasive, and obviously positive, influence on the structural evolution and location of contemporary US industry (Stein 1985, pp. 345-8; Smith 1987, p. 4). In the second alternative it is argued that, in the main, military technology and expenditures have been largely irrelevant for the US economy. Its contribution "appears to depend on the kind of technology and the economic setting in which the invention is occurring" (Adams and Gold 1987, p. 291). The third possibility is, of course, that military industry is at the root of the US economic decline.

In order to explore the relationship between the development of military technology and its civilian economic consequences both a general exploratory analysis and a case study are needed. In the general context my starting point is that both the deceleration of productivity growth and the relative scarcity of commercially useful innovations erode the competitive capacity of the US economy, even though they do not determine it. In both cases military spending, and in particular its use to develop and acquire weapons systems, should be considered a potential *explanandum* of the relative economic decline of the United States. The model of explanation has to be rather complex, however, as the empirical evidence that the military burden is discouraging economic development is ambiguous and certainly not always compelling.

It is quite easy to develop a theoretical argument, underpinned by some empirical evidence, that military R&D is diverting resources from the development of civilian technological innovations, distorting the industrial structure and reducing the competitiveness of the economy by slowing down productivity growth. In particular, military spending appears to slow down capital investment and, for that reason, the growth and restructuring of the economy, while its other economic correlates have not been established equally firmly (deGrasse 1984; Lindgren 1988).

Indeed, correlations between various measures of the military effort and economic change are often insignificant. A systematic review of research suggests that there has hardly been either negative or positive long-term correlation between military and civilian R&D spending. Furthermore, a minimum of 60 per cent of the productivity slowdown is caused by variables other than changes in R&D (Adams and Gold 1987, pp. 272-7; Gold 1990, pp. 29-44).

Somewhat paradoxically, the US military allocations have a stronger impact on the private sector than on the public one. It is obvious that in technical terms military expenditures have not affected the federal budget any more than other types of spending. The budget deficits have been created by the consistent increase in domestic spending overall and not by military expenditures alone. Federal budget expenditures have continued to grow as a kind of secular trend despite the temporary reductions in the relative military spending (Nau 1990, pp. 337-8). It has been estimated that in the 1980s the borrowing of the federal government absorbed nearly three-quarters of the total net savings in the United States. The absence of funds for investment has restricted productivity growth and industrial employment (Friedman 1990, pp. 29-30).

No doubt the US budget deficits in the 1980s would have been smaller if military expenditure had been cut back or had remained constant during the Reagan years instead of more money being pumped into it. Yet, it cannot be regarded as the root cause of the growth and imbalance in the federal budget. Neither has military expenditure directly hampered the growth of federal spending for educational and health purposes; their problems have to be traced to other factors. In 1941-79 no systematic and statistically significant trade-off between military and welfare spending existed (Russett 1982). On the contrary, it has been suggested that the "military budget . . . is really a part of the particular late-twentieth-century American version of the welfare state" (Friedman 1990, pp. 31-2).

Military allocations, as any other categories of public expenditure, tend to crowd out both personal consumption and investment, even though specific interactions vary from one country and time period to another. There is considerable evidence on the negative relationship between capital investment and military spending (Lindgren 1985, pp. 9-11; Adams and Gold 1987, pp. 273-4). This evidence is based primarily on cross-sectional data and bivariate correlations. Countrywise diachronic analyses between military spending and investment on the one hand and multivariate analyses on the other might yield different results.

A relevant trend to observe here is that the composition of US military spending has significantly changed and it differs increasingly from the non-military government expenditure. In 1984 only 8 per cent of the non-military spending went to buy durable goods, while the corresponding share for the military spending was 48 per cent and has been increasing over time. With the change in the structure of the US economy both the non-military public spending and private spending are increasingly used to purchase services, while military expenditure is allocated to buy capital goods whose share in the GNP is otherwise declining. Moreover, the military funds go to a limited set of industries, primarily to heavy manufacturing industries (Blank and Rothschild 1985, pp. 678-85).

This would not necessarily be bad if the military spending would enhance investment in the capital goods industry and in that way improve the industrial backbone of the economy. In fact, it has been suggested that the US federal government has a closet industrial policy implemented by the Pentagon through a variety of organizational arrangements such as the Defense Advanced Research Projects Agency (DARPA) and the Office of Economic Adjustment. The Strategic Defense Initiative (SDI) and the Strategic Computing Initiative (SCI) have been identified as practical manifestations of the Pentagon's effort to bolster the strength and productivity of the US economy by allocating military spending to R&D projects which also have a long-term commercial potential. The Pentagon's industrial policy has often been considered, along with the demand management, a paramount example of the "military Keynesianism". In particular, DARPA has funded over the years a wide range of projects in critical technologies (Junne 1985; Markusen 1986, pp. 496-9, 505-7; Lucas 1990, pp. 94-7; Kuttner 1991, pp. 212-18).

The relative emphasis on the capital goods industry in the allocation of military procurement funds calls for some further exploration here. A long-term trend appears to be that high-tech industries are replacing heavy industries, such as steel, machinery and construction, as targets of military funds. The heavy industries are thus increasingly dependent on public investment in the maintenance of their infrastructure, which has been badly neglected in the United States since the 1960s. Apart from its potential positive consequences the strengthening linkage between military spending and high-tech industries may increase the economic problems of the United States by undermining industrial employment and contributing to the unevenness of regional economic performance (Markusen 1986, pp. 499-503).

In principle, the military interest in the new core technologies such as microelectronics and telecommunications could give rise to such products and production processes that are at the edge of the present industrial revolution. These technology clusters have a potential not only to create new commercially viable products, but more importantly to renew industrial organization and its modes of operation by increasing efficiency and flexibility (van Tulder and Junne 1988; Lucas 1990, pp. 98-102). Because of the crucial nature of this issue it will be scrutinized further in a case study concerning the semiconductor industry, which is developing and producing one of the new core technologies.

There is a measure of futility in the exploration of the relationship between military spending and economic decline at too high a level of generality. Instead, the relationship must be specified in order to gain more valid answers. The analysis above shows that the potential trade-offs of military spending have to be traced to the private sector rather than to the federal budget, and in particular to the investments in R&D and the manufacturing industries. It is well known that military expenditure is allocated to a handful of industries controlled by a very few large companies. The economic impact is obviously mediated through these industries and firms. Science and technology appear to be in a pivotal intermediary position between military production and economic development.

As a starting point for the analysis, one may recall that the extensive investment of resources in science and technology during World War II, together with the import of European specialists in the 1930s and again after 1945, spurred significant technological advances. Both during and after World War II the amount and productivity of the US industrial production were augmented significantly (Cohen and Wilson 1988, p. 117; Porter 1990, pp. 294-9). There was a close linkage between military R&D allocations to individual industries and their relevance for the military. The growth of federal R&D, starting in the middle of the 1950s, coincides with the onset of the technological arms race. The expanding federal R&D funds went to aircraft and missiles, electrical equipment, and machinery and motor vehicles, and these sectors also absorbed the bulk of all R&D resources. In these sectors military R&D accounted, respectively, for 90, 60 and 25 per cent of all R&D expenditure (Mansfield 1980, pp. 570-1).

Perhaps a crucial feature of the early postwar period was that the allocation of R&D funds for military purposes went to the core technologies:

A large defense programme was instrumental in promoting science and in creating advanced home demand. In the 1940s, 1950s and 1960s, defense research centered on core technologies such as electronics, computers, and aerospace. Commercial spin-offs were numerous and rapid. With a huge technological lead in fields serving defense and aerospace markets, US companies often exploited their knowledge and experience to establish leading positions in the civilian markets. (Porter 1990, p. 305)

The critical linkage, mediated by the military interests, between R&D and core technologies operated as long as the United States was in a hegemonic economic position. When the relative decline of this position started in the middle of the 1960s, the military technological programmes had a "resulting penalty to new commercial processes and products and to industrial productivity" (Mettler 1980, p. 600). This tendency has obviously been reinforced by the highly classified, "black" programmes, and in general by military secrecy and organizational barriers, which have prevented the commercial applications of military technologies produced in them (Defense Technology Base 1988, p. 11).

Technological leadership was a part of the hegemonic system established by the United States after World War II. This leadership was "both a symbol of economic power and, dependent as it had been on defence R&D, a symbol of defence strength as well. To lose leadership in electronics was to lose defence as well as economic virility" (Hills 1983, p. 222). The change seems to have happened in the middle of the 1960s when the military contribution to the development of civilian goods for the competitive market went into decline. This trend has continued until today; military R&D is falling behind civilian research especially in electronics and the military sector has come to rely on advances in civilian research programmes (Carey 1991, p. 99).

The relative decline of the US economic position and the lagging behind of the military electronics industry have eroded the critical historical linkage between military R&D and core technologies. The R&D funds go, it is true, to industries which are highly dependent on advanced technologies such as missiles and space systems as well as electronic and communication systems. Together they account for more than 60 per cent of all the military R&D in the United States (Chesnais *et al.* 1990, p. 12). Another source estimates that in 1988 the combined share of aerospace, electronics and telecommunication in the total military R&D was 79 per cent, about the same as in 1957 (Derian 1990, pp. 44-5). No doubt there have been commercial spin-offs in these high-tech sectors, while other fields, including consumer goods, have hardly benefited from military spending (Stowsky 1986, p. 701).

The relative economic decline of the United States correlates thus with the inability to commercialize the technologies developed by the Department of Defense (DoD) funding. This is largely due to the "sheltered culture" of arms manufacturers. The military requirements of the DoD and the requirements of the civilian market diverged increasingly from the middle of the 1960's onwards. While the military contractors were able to develop technologies relevant for civilian needs, their contribution was limited. Most innovations for the market, for instance in electronics, came from the companies which did not collaborate with the Pentagon or had initiated such a relationship only recently. Their competitiveness in the market was derived from their ability to conduct self-financed R&D and, in that way, to stay clear of the institutional constraints imposed by the DoD (Derian 1990, pp. 139-43).

Even the military has become concerned for the state of the defence industry. The existing relationship between arms manufacturing and industrial-technological advance is revealed by the DoD concern over the "antiquated and inefficient manufacturing practices within the defense industries". Where modernization has been accomplished, the focus has been on complex high-tech systems, which has led to "shortfalls in manufacturing technologies" (Defense Technology Base 1988, p. 50). These problems plague, in the first place, the prime contractors of weapons systems that account for about one-half of the money allocated to such systems. The rest of it is further channelled to subcontractors and parts suppliers. However, this lower tier has been shrinking and has become more concentrated, which creates bottlenecks and delivery problems. Also the innovative technological input of small companies and their spin-off potential are often lost (Gansler 1980, pp. 128-32; Gansler 1989, pp. 257-63).

An increasing share of the military spending thus goes to the production of capital goods in which the availability of public money has reduced the propensity of companies to invest themselves in the industrial plants and technology. The private R&D funds have been allocated, in part, to other than heavy manufacturing industries - for example, electronics. This trend has exacerbated the problems from which the smokestack industries have generally been suffering and has given a chance to other countries with more efficient capital goods industries to expand their global market share.

A consequence of the weakening of the manufacturing base in the United States has been its growing dependence on foreign supplies of critical technologies. The US weapons systems are increasingly dependent on foreign micro-electronics and special materials needed in optics, computers and other military equipment. For example, in special silicon, random access memories (RAMs), fibre optics products and liquid crystal displays US dependency on foreign suppliers is nearly total. Approximately one-half of the advanced electronics used in the US weapons systems are imported from Japan and the share is growing. During the last few years there have been signs that the US government has opted increasingly for a techno-nationalist position which encourages domestic production of critical technologies and curbs their exports. Such a policy may not be feasible anymore, however, and may, in fact, have counter-productive effects on the national economic development (Gansler 1989, pp. 271-3; Haglund and Busch 1989; Moran 1990).

The Semiconductor Industry

As promised earlier, the interplay of military production and industrial dynamics will be explored by a case study focusing on the semiconductor industry. It is a crucial rather than a representative case; one may not be able to generalize from it, but it supposedly provides clues to the impact of military procurement on the rise and evolution of new industries. Of course, the semiconductor industry is not the only potential object of the case study. The machine-tool industry, especially the production of numerically controlled tools, would be another possibility. The military interest in machine tools has existed for over a century; in fact, military requirements initiated the machine-tool industry, which then contributed to the mechanization of a variety of civilian industries (Smith 1987, pp. 77-9). With the escalation of the technological arms race, the weapons industry has become increasingly dependent on the sophistication of numerically controlled machines. Yet, the impact of the military demand on the industry, if any, must have been qualitative rather than quantitative since it accounts for only 20 per cent of its total production (Gould 1990, p. 49).

In the United States the numerical control of production was inaugurated by the air force in order to improve the performance of aircraft and missiles and to increase its control of the industrial plants. The investment of military funds in the development of numerical control forced hesitant companies to participate and to create a system which was complex, costly and unreliable, and which killed technical and organizational alternatives. The focus on performance and specialization made perfect sense for the air force, but undermined at the same time the commercial competitiveness of the US machine manufacturers. This trend was reinforced by the concentration of German and Japanese companies on cheaper, simpler and more accessible designs which were commercially feasible (Noble 1987, pp. 340-5; Gansler 1989, pp. 89-90).

It has been suggested that the main weaknesses of the US industry of numerically controlled machine tools has been the heavy fluctuation in demand, the small size of companies involved and the consequent undercapitalization (diFilippo 1986). Thus the ability to introduce new commercial technologies has been limited and can be contrasted with the Japanese determination to raise funds and systematically to strengthen the production of machine tools; by 1986 Japan had become their largest producer in the world. At that time, the United States imported one-half of its requirement for machine tools, compared with twenty years earlier when it had been almost self-sufficient. (Gould 1990, p. 46).

It has been argued, especially with reference to the Houdaille company, that the decline of the US industry was mainly caused in the competitive market by the public subsidies to the Japanese machine tool industry (Prestowitz 1988, pp. 217-29). This interpretation has been contested, however, by pointing out that the takeover mania, the ineptitude of the federal bureaucracy and the ill-advised economic policies of the Reagan Administration were more important than Japanese competition in bringing down the US machine tool industry (Holland 1989).

The military was certainly not the only culprit in the decline of the US machine tool industry. The inability of the US producers to keep the costs under the lid, the lack of R&D funds for civilian projects and the failure to develop products for the civilian market may all be traced back to the subordination of civilian to military priorities in the industry (diFilippo 1986). Hence the role of the military has not been the sole influential factor and there is evidence that a variety of other factors had an impact on the decline of the industry in the United States. For instance, the symbiotic relationship between the Japanese machine tool industry and the manufacturers of durable goods has shielded the industry from the vagaries of the market and has pulled it to the new frontiers of technology.

In contrast, in the United States the machine tool industry has been more isolated from the manufacturers and has not been activated by their demand (Gould 1990, pp.

45-54; Gould 1991, pp. 40-1). Related evidence on the impact of military interests and foreign competition on individual industries and their technological trajectories could be gained from the ball-bearing and precision-gear industries (Haglund and Busch 1989, pp. 249-50).

Semiconductors have been at the edge of technical innovation and, as "brain cells" of high-technology products, they have a multitude of important civilian and military uses. For this reason the semiconductor business provides ample material for a crucial case study on the economic effects of the production of advanced, militarily relevant technology. The significance of military electronics can be seen in the fact that of the 20 biggest US arms-producing companies 75 per cent were involved in 1988 in electronics. Among the 50 biggest arms manufacturers the corresponding share is 67 per cent (calculated from Anthony *et al.* 1990, pp. 326-8).

A significant phase in the development of the transistor was inaugurated in 1946 when Bell Laboratories were able to replace bulky vacuum tubes by it. Right from the beginning the US military, especially the Army Signal Corps, was interested in the potential uses of the transistor. Its activities had a profound impact on the development and dissemination of the transistor: "By sponsoring application studies, organizing bureaus for production development and disseminating the new technology to industry, the military assumed responsibility for presiding over the process of technological development and hence began its activities as an institutional entrepreneur in this new field" (Misa 1985, p. 268).

The rapid progress in semiconductor technology continued in the 1950s and the 1960s. In 1959 Texas Instruments invented the integrated circuit and in 1968 Intel Corporation devised the dynamic random access memory (DRAM). The pace of innovation continued to be swift and in 1971 Intel developed the microprocessor, a chip with large memory and capacity. The capacity of RAM also expanded: 4K RAM in 1973, 16K RAM in 1975 and 64K RAM in 1980. In general, it can be said that most new steps in the semiconductor industry originated from large companies, although their complementarity with small firms was also important (Derian 1990, pp. 31-2).

The interest of the military in the semiconductor industry is not surprising at all. A main advantage of the semiconductors stems from their integrated character; instead of carrying a discrete circuit, as transistors do, the semiconductors contain an integrated circuit of several electronic devices which are pressed on semiconductive material such as silicon. Semiconductors facilitate the miniaturization of parts, greater capacity of information processing and lower power consumption, all of which are desirable properties in military equipment.

The support of the Defense Department for the emerging semiconductor industry was extensive and even decisive; in 1963 government procurement accounted for 95 per cent of sales. By 1966 the volume of the US semiconductor market was multiplied by twenty to $80 million, and the government share was 75 per cent. Even though the production of semiconductors for the civilian market had expanded from $0.2 million to $20 million, demand from that market was not able to shoulder the heavy costs of development and production. Many contracts were concluded between the Defense Department and companies to develop integrated circuits for military and space applications (Stowsky 1986, pp. 702-4).

Although there were efforts to spread the new technology to the companies, through the system known as second-sourcing and in other ways, there is evidence of the conflict between the needs of the military and the civilian market. This tension was faced also by Bell Telephone Laboratories which in the 1950s originally developed the transistor for the telephone system, but in which field its use was precluded by military interests for over a decade. The development of technology for military purposes advanced uniform national standards, but these standards and, more importantly, the specific technological requirements of the military differed so much from the commercial needs that its introduction to the market was slow and cumbersome (Misa 1985, pp. 285-7).

In the 1970s tension between the Defense Department and the semiconductor industry increased as the latter wanted to orient more to the civilian market. There were several reasons for this tension. The rapid decrease in the costs of producing microchips enhanced the importance of the economies of scale to be achieved from the commercial market and reduced the role of military demand. The military R&D produced few basic technological innovations, partly because of the lack of funding for basic research, and partly because most of the funds went to large electronics manufacturers. Their bureaucratic organization was probably less conducive to technological innovations than that of small companies, had the latter received comparable funding (deGrasse 1983, pp. 106-14).

The tension between military and commercial uses could be coped with as long as it remained domestic, that is, as long as there were no foreign competitors worthy of mention. This was the case until about the end of the 1970s. In 1975 the Japanese share of the world market of DRAMs was 10 per cent and of SRAMs (static RAM) 2 per cent. By 1978 these shares had increased to 24 and 15 per cent respectively, while in the case of EPROMs (electrical, programmable read-only memory) the corresponding share was 4 per cent. Thereafter, US leadership in the semiconductor market was quickly eroded and disappeared altogether by the mid-1980s. In 1986 the Japanese share of the world market of both DRAMs and SRAMs was 80 per cent and of EPROMs 52 per cent. The rest of the market was shared by the US and European semiconductor companies (Chesnais *et al.* 1990, pp. 48-9).

The rapid change in the world market of the memory chips can be illustrated by the race for the 64K RAM. In the early 1970s the Japanese decided to challenge the United States, or more precisely the IBM leadership, in the development of computers utilizing the RAM chips. In 1976 the MITI launched, under the aegis of the NTT, a consortium of major computer companies that was to strengthen the Japanese semiconductor industry by plunging directly into the development of advanced RAMs. Work on the Very Large Scale Integration (VLSI) technology, financed extensively by public money and aided by various restrictive business practices, progressed rapidly.

In 1978 the first Japanese 16K RAMs came to the international market and soon had a 40 per cent share. In early 1980 the Japanese beat IBM by introducing, ahead of it, the new 64K RAM to the market. Later on in the same year NTT announced that it had developed the first prototype of the 256K RAM (Prestowitz 1988, pp. 35-9; Derian 1990, pp. 125-7). The Japanese advances in quality, productivity and cost reduction in the VLSI programme "exceeded all expectations. By 1980 Japanese companies had surpassed US merchant semiconductor firms in the design and manufacture of the latest generation of semiconductor devices" (Inman and Burton 1990, p. 119).

These US merchant firms - first of all Intel, Motorola and Texas Instruments - had been competing with each other, and they were now beaten by the consortium of Toshiba, Fujitsu, Sony, Hitachi and other Japanese semiconductor companies. The Americans have usually blamed the Japanese for their use of unfair trading practices and subsidies to the domestic industry. In addition, the US fears were heightened by the planned takeover by Fujitsu of Fairchild Semiconductor Company. In the end, the takeover was blocked by the Reagan Administration (Haglund and Busch 1989, pp. 251-3).

The real story is more complicated, however, and shows how the Japanese companies did not utilize extensively or benefit from "dirty tricks", but meticulously developed their commercial and technological acumen. For instance, in 1953 Sony licenced the solid-state transistor technology from Western Electric and, after having improved it for consumer needs, gradually captured the market. Similarly, many other US electronics firms have experienced a process of relative decline in the market and have concluded strategic alliances with their Japanese counterparts. Such alliances sometimes elicit criticism, but the Americans have no other alternative than to continue inter-company co-operation. Often the Japanese companies dominate in the strategic alliances, but IBM is an exception; globally it has more than 40 alliances and it has successfully penetrated the Japanese economy (Ohmae 1990, p. 131).

The Japanese success has been based principally on two factors. The members of the NTT consortium had "patient", low-interest money for their long-term capital investment and a secure market of other Japanese companies purchasing memory products. Another relevant factor has been the Japanese recognition that the RAM, which is the first to incorporate the newest technology, is the keystone of the entire semiconductor industry. The Japanese, in other words, "knew that if they could capture the lead in RAMs, they would be well on the way to overall semiconductor superiority" (Prestowitz 1988, p. 40). Cheap capital, the expanding scale of production and outright dumping helped the Japanese companies to become low-cost producers and to conquer a growing share of the market (Prestowitz 1988, pp. 42-6). The support they gained from the Japanese government was hardly critical (Derian 1990, p. 173).

More recent experience can be obtained from the VLSIs with increased chip density and computation speed, which makes their price more competitive. In Japan, the VLSI project was launched in 1976. Close to one-half of the total funds of $300 million came from the state budget and the rest from the corporate coalitions which joined the project. This project has been held up as a good example of how in Japan the state plays a commanding role in the development of new competitive technologies. Furthermore, the companies are said to suppress their mutual competition when the task is to develop technologies in order to capture market shares. In reality, there were constraints in Japan on both the role of the state and intra-industry co-operation, and these factors were less effective than is usually imagined (Fong 1990, pp. 283-7, 294; cf. Inman and Burton 1990, p. 120).

In the United States the VLSI technology was sponsored in the main by the Department of Defense which launched, in its quest for a technological force multiplier and to regain control over the semiconductor industry, the Very High Speed Integrated Circuit Programme (VHSIC). DARPA was actively involved in the project to which companies from the commercial market were also brought in. The programme covered the period 1980-88 and had a total price tag of $1 billion - a major programme, indeed. In one judgement, "VHSIC represented America's largest, most ambitious government initiative in microelectronics in decades" (Fong 1990, pp. 278-80; Chesnais *et al.* 1990, pp. 51-4).

The VHSIC initiative was inspired by the recognition in the Department of Defense that the military applications of semiconductors were jeopardized by the commercial interests. That is why companies from the commercial sector were brought into the programme under the control of the Department of Defense, whose central role meant that the technological requirements were redefined to favour military needs. Chips were custom-made, rather than produced in large quantities and at small cost. In addition, secrecy and export restrictions curbed the commercial utilization of the chips (Stowsky 1986, pp. 710-12; Derian 1990, pp. 143-4).

Both arms manufacturers (Rockwell, Honeywell, Raytheon, and others) and commercial semiconductor companies (Texas Instruments, Motorola and National Semiconductor, but not Intel) were initially interested in VHSIC. The main reason for this interest was the complementarity between VHSIC technology and the mainstream commercial technology. Even though the companies, oriented to the open civilian market, did not like the military restrictions embedded in the projects, they expected the commercial benefits to be high enough to warrant their participation. They were disappointed by the meagre results. Yet VHSIC opened a new chapter in government-industry co-operation in an industry whose structure has been fluid and fragmented (Fong 1990, pp. 288-90; Chesnais *et al.* 1990, pp. 57-8). In the end, the worrying question remains whether or not the VHSIC programme has, in reality, undermined rather than strengthened the commercial competitiveness of US semiconductor companies in comparison with Japanese firms.

Concluding Remarks

What, then, has been the role of the military interests in the US loss of pivotal high-tech areas to Japanese competition? While it is impossible to provide any definitive answers a few tentative observations can be made. One of them concerns the insulation of the US military industry from the international market. Until recently it has been deliberately nurtured by the Department of Defense and reinforced by the decoupling of the military industry from the commercial manufacturers. This means that the military technology, which has been overspecified and overtested in comparison with the needs of the civilian market, has gradually started lagging behind the civilian technology. For example, RAMs for the commercial market are rather easy and cheap to improve, while the custom chips for the military are more costly to design and have less spin-off potential for commercial applications. This has tended to decelerate the growth of the civilian RAM market, which, in turn, worried semiconductor companies and prompted them to increase their autonomy and even antagonism towards the DoD (Stowsky 1986, pp. 706-7; Fong 1990, pp. 282-3).

Indeed, the issue of the decoupling of military industry from commercial reality appears to be critical here. The problem may not be the direct negative impact of military spending, R&D and production on the US economy so such as the separation, measured by the number and nature of technological spin-offs, of civilian and military production from each other. Military spending has not inspired the development of competitive products and efficient production technologies, in particular, for the consumer goods market, but has instead served the specific military needs. The civilian products, to the extent they have emerged from the diversification of military manufacturers into new areas, have often turned out to be "quasi-weapons systems" rather than genuine civilian versions (Kaldor 1981, p. 195, 221-2; see also Stowsky 1986, pp. 700-1).

The self-encapsulation of the military has been associated with the relative decline in the efficiency of the military industry and the low pace of its commercialization. For instance, in the US semiconductor industry the main problem has not been the lack of technological innovation, but the "inability to bring new technology rapidly to the market and to manufacture high-quality products" (Inman and Burton 1990, p. 120). This problem has been due both to the technological style of the military industry and to its secrecy and restrictions on the transfer of technology.

During the Reagan build-up in the first half of the 1980s, the contractors became more dependent on the military programmes, especially in the aerospace industry. In some industries this increased the total output, but in others it decreased in spite of the growth of military purchases (Henry and Oliver 1987, pp. 4-7). The increase in the dependence of manufacturing firms on military contractors did not solve the problem of decoupling, however. On the contrary, it tended to isolate further the military contractors from the civilian market by tying them to the Department of Defense, and to undermine their ability to commercialize their products and to reach out to the civilian market.

The relative economic decline of the United States and the decoupling of the military industries from the commercial market are obviously connected with each other. During the period of US economic hegemony, military R&D and production encouraged commercial high-tech industries, including aircraft production, satellite communications, fibre optics and computers (Gold 1991, p. 41). The United States could afford to fund both military and civilian technology projects that also interacted with each other. The high level of military spending was "affordable because the economy was strong, military spending contributed significantly to commercial technologies and military procurement was technologically efficient" (Ferguson 1986).

With the relative decline of US economic capabilities this positive equation is now in jeopardy. While the military spending boom in the 1950s and the 1960s encouraged technological development, its impact in the different circumstances of the 1980s seems to have been reversed (Hall and Preston 1988, pp. 279-80). This is due, in part, to the egoistic character of the military industry that has led to the build-up of "ever more islands of industry that exist strictly to supply the military. And the military market is not large enough to enable real experience-curve economies" (Prestowitz 1988, p. 248).

The same problem has also been formulated in terms of the weakening of the "dual-use infrastructure of domestic technology". This suggests that the present interplay of the military and civilian industries is not able to produce the leading-edge technologies that the United States considers it needs in the military competition with its adversaries (Defense Technology Base 1988, pp. 42-6). That is why military officials have argued that national security requires an intensified commitment of civilian manufacturing technology to the production of military hardware and software. Such a commitment is particularly needed in the electronics industry (Kuttner 1991, pp. 221-4).

The process of decoupling between civilian and military industries is taking place in the changing international context; the world technological system is increasingly global, dynamic and competitive. With a few exceptions, the US companies have not been overtly successful in competing for market share in the high-tech industries. On the contrary, their relative influence has decreased and the country has been converted into a net importer in many categories of advanced technologies. Thus, while the US civilian industries have failed largely for their own reasons, the military industry, increasingly isolated and inefficient, is not able to fill the gap and is becoming a drag on the overall industrial strength (Ferguson 1986; Prestowitz 1988, pp. 246-9).

In order to arrest the US relative economic decline and to improve the technological preconditions for top military performance, a two-pronged strategy has been recommended and, to a degree, implemented. Such a strategy makes the hitherto covert industrial policy of the Department of Defense more explicit. One of its elements is to increase the productivity and efficiency of the military industry by creating new incentives to move in this direction. Another objective has been to integrate the civilian and military production more closely with each other (Gansler 1987, pp. 57-9; Gansler 1989, pp. 273-82). To pursue an industrial strategy along these lines the Department of Defense has initiated new policies and institutional arrangements.

In the field of semiconductors, the establishment of Sematech (Semiconductor Manufacturing Technology Corporation), a public/private venture, is a concrete sign of this effort. The Sematech project covers the period 1988-93 and costs a total of $1 billion (Pianta 1988, p. 95; Inman and Burton 1990, pp. 120-1). Sematech is intended both to improve the military performance by fostering relevant new technologies and to help to commercialize them.

The general conclusion that emerges from my analysis is that the relative economic decline of the United States has not, in the first place, been due to the military spending, R&D and production. The long-term convergence of the levels of economic prosperity and productivity in the United States and its economic challengers can be accounted for by the general catch-up logic of economic and industrial development (Abramovitz 1986; Gold 1990, pp. 75-81). The economic and technological effects of military allocations are not unimportant, however.

Military spending does not prevent economic growth, but it necessarily becomes a drag. Being relatively protected and inefficient in government custody, the military industry absorbs a part of the national wealth which does not enter effectively into economic circulation. The economy can stand such an amputation as long as it is, in relative terms, internationally dominant. Once the undisputed international leadership has gone, the extensive military allocations, inherited from the previous period of dominance, become increasingly a burden unless the efficiency of military industry is significantly improved and the spin-off process begins to operate.

So far the economic burden created by the military has been coped with in the United States, although with increasing difficulties. The next upturn in the long economic wave will be decisive for the United States; "productive leadership in the system will then depend on who wins and who loses that upturn" (Thompson 1990, p. 232). As the probability of a general war remains low and there is no combined economic and military challenge to its leadership, the US power position will not rapidly wither away. That is why the transition to the new power constellation will be gradual and the struggle will take place in the economic sphere, and in particular, in the command of leading-edge technologies and productive resources. There are different views on whether the United States will be able to reverse its decline during the coming upturn, if it ever comes (for example, Rosecrance 1990, pp. 61-5).

The challenge has been understood by the US economic and political elite. It is more and more often pointed out that military policy cannot be made by military criteria or foreign policy by diplomatic criteria alone. Instead, the economic factors, in particular the preservation of US economic leadership, are vital in the formulation of its foreign and military policy (Inman and Burton 1990, p. 134; Cohen and Wilson 1988). The accumulation of military power has become, economically speaking, too costly, and has to be tailored in the future to the productive and technological imperatives in order to survive in international competition with Japan and the European Community.

Chapter 5
Brazil: Military Industrialization
and Technological Autonomy

History of Military Industry

As in any other country, the emergence and consolidation of the Brazilian military industry can only be understood in the context of its overall economic and social development. In the course of its history, Brazil has had recurrent military conflicts with its neighbours, in particular with Argentina, Uruguay and Paraguay. Yet it is justified to argue that Brazil's military industry has not grown out of its external security needs so much as from its expansionist policy of national development.

Brazil has a systematic record of geopolitical expansion to the interior of South America. This historic expansion has been shaped both by politico-military interests and commodity cycles by which the economic development has leaped forward. Military capabilities have been used as instruments of this expansion. In addition, they have been a means of consolidating Brazil's huge but fragile geographical empire which extends from La Plata to the Amazon frontier (Branco 1983; Väyrynen 1989).

The first steps to build up the Brazilian military industry were taken in the nineteenth century, when the first plants to produce small arms and ammunition were established. The extent of arms production remained very modest, however. The lack of military-industrial dynamics in Brazil can be traced back to its position in the international centre-periphery structure. Its external dependence was visible in the export of primary products and in the import of manufactured goods (Frank 1969, pp. 190-4). Without the domestic capital goods industry the indigenous production of arms cannot be started. Such a start calls, in turn, for political determination to increase the economic autonomy of the country.

The need of an indigenous arms industry was more widely recognized during the Old Republic (1889-1930). The level of military spending remained relatively low, however, during the last two decades of the nineteenth century. In 1896 the share of military spending of the state budget jumped from some 17 per cent to 25 per cent and to more than 30 per cent at the turn of the century (Banks 1982, p. 103). This increase was obviously associated with the possibility of a major armed confrontation with Argentina, which led the political leadership to advocate strongly a greater national self-sufficiency in arms production. This motivation was compounded by the difficulty in acquiring weapons from the international arms market during World War I. Before World War I Brazil imported most of the military hardware it needed, in particular from Germany (Hilton 1982, pp. 629-34; Branco 1983, pp. 259-60). The dependence was strong enough to warrant McCann to speak in this context of the "germanization of the Brazilian army" in the early twentieth century (McCann 1984, pp. 742 and 747).

The achievement of a greater autonomy in munitions production was declared as the most immediate goal. However, this was only a beginning; a much higher degree of military-industrial autonomy was sought by the Brazilian government (Hilton 1982, pp. 638-41). Indeed, in the early twentieth century, the plans for an indigenous military industry were closely co-ordinated with the general industrial policy. Economic strength was declared as a precondition for national security and coherence. Thus, failure in international economic competition would have adverse political consequences for national security.

The utilization of domestic coal and iron deposits was motivated by the need to build railways and naval vessels. In the uncertain conditions of World War I, the extensive foreign control of Brazil's strategic railways and its dependence on arms imports gave rise to the idea of establishing a national steel industry. Brazil's steel industry was therefore born out of the state-sponsored amalgamation of military needs and the requirements of long-term industrial development (Hilton 1982, pp. 642-3; Topik 1979, pp. 338-9; McCann 1984, pp. 760-1).

Underpinning this "military-industrial complex" there was a conviction that "national greatness was linked to military preparedness, which in turn depended upon the country's economic development" (McCann 1984, p. 737). The long story of Brazil's steel industry, culminating in 1946 in the opening of the Volta Redonda plant, is in many ways instructive. The story shows how the industry was inspired by the nationalist frustration with dependence on foreign steel and the expansion of European mining companies to Brazil's iron ore fields (Wirth 1970, pp. 71-89).

The 1920s was a decade of economic crisis in Brazil, permitting few opportunities of expanding military procurement. The army was ill-equipped, the navy was in primitive shape and the air force almost non-existent. The condition of external dependence is illustrated by the efforts in the 1920s of the European and, later on, the US aircraft manufacturers to penetrate the South American market. The emphasis was on commercial aircraft, but military sales were also promoted (Newton 1965).

During the Old Republic there was much political and professional debate on the need to establish a domestic arms industry, but few results. However, the debate helped, as Stanley Hilton has pointed out, to create a

> growing realization of the need for greater defense modernization and autonomy. It was also during that period that important questions about defense production were first raised and supplied answers that, by and large, would satisfy the ensuing generations. That more was not accomplished was the result primarily of factors beyond governmental control. The take-off in military production and military-civilian industrial co-operation had to await increased centralization of political authority, the onset of true industrialization, and the recruitment of broader sectors of the political and industrial elites to the cause of military autonomy. (Hilton 1982, p. 646)

These developments received a new impetus in 1930 when, in the aftermath of the 1929 crash, Getulio Vargas overthrew the old republican political order and established a new corporatist *Estado Nôvo*. It was a counter-reaction to the political and economic structure of the Old Republic. Vargas's *golpe de estado* strove for the establishment of a strong central government which passed social welfare legislation and organized the labour in syndicalist fashion. This arrangement was intended to underpin political stability and to create a government-labour pact that would support *Estado Nôvo*'s programme of national industrialization and build a political edifice.

Vargas's policy was based on economic nationalism which favoured public investment and other forms of state intervention in the critical sectors of the economy. This policy of state-directed industrialization was a response to the realization that Brazil's traditional economic structure had collapsed and could not be brought back to life. The military supported, and to a degree initiated, *Estado Nôvo*'s state-directed industrialization strategy in Brazil, especially in sectors which were essential for national security (Skidmore 1967, pp. 43-7).

The strong commitment of the military to the establishment of a national steel industry is a case in point. According to Wirth (1970, p. 89) "the Army was determined to establish a steelworks as one of its primary goals in the Estado Nôvo". Although admitting the long-term interest of the top military leaders in the promotion of heavy industry, Hilton (1973, pp. 85-6) draws a different conclusion and stresses the importance of civilian agents both in establishing the Volta Redonda steelworks and in the general industrialization of Brazil by state intervention.

Industrialization produces tangible results only over a long term. That is why the steps taken in the 1930s in the military industrialization of Brazil only modestly helped the armed forces, which remained dependent on foreign purchases. Yet the planning and construction of military industries was started in Brazil: government planning commissions were established, the production of small arms and ammunition was expanded, the shipbuilding industry launched minesweepers, and the assembly of aircraft was initiated. There were, however, several bottlenecks in arms manufacturing: scarcity of financial resources and the lack of technical expertise were the most serious ones. To eliminate the latter problem, the Escola Técnica was established in 1930 and Brazilian technicians and officers were sent to foreign companies for training (Hilton 1982, pp. 654-6).

The expansion of military production in Brazil has to be interpreted within the prevailing internal and external contexts. The economic stagnation of the 1930s opened to the *Estado Nôvo* new possibilities for fostering developmental capitalism, for reducing its dependence on the United States and for expanding relations with the Third Reich (Frank 1969, pp. 204-8). The expansion of German-Brazilian economic relations was due to a variety of factors: ideological affinities, the lack of alternatives in the external economic policy of Brazil, and the compatibility of bilateral compensation deals with its model of economic development, all played their role.

To quell the opposition of the conservative political forces and to eliminate the dissatisfaction of the military made it necessary for the Vargas government to prop up the federal military, which was rather weak in comparison with various military forces in the states. The domestic political imperative illustrates one pertinent problem of the Brazilian military. Ostensibly it is supposed to defend the country against external attacks, but in reality its primary mission has been internal: to keep the opposition forces under control and to consolidate, together with other branches of the state, the vast, socially and territorially divided country (McCann 1980).

In the 1930s, the domestic policy also spilled over into external relations: "military unrest over the inadequate material conditions of the armed forces, and translation of that discontent into pressure for matériel, became a key component of decision-making on foreign trade policy" (Hilton 1973, pp. 77-8). The scarcity of foreign exchange made the German and Italian offers to barter weapons for cotton and coffee a lucrative offer for the Brazilians. In 1937 Krupp concluded, on a compensation basis, a major contract in Brazil's rearmament programme (Hilton 1973, pp. 79-84). In fact, these economic and military ties made Brazil an overseas participant of Germany's closed *Wirtschaftsraum*. In Brazil, material deficiencies and the fear of instabilities "forged an alliance between the high command and commercial bilateralism" (Hilton 1973, pp. 89-90).

In the prewar Brazil there was an observable difference between the reality and the vision. In reality, the economic structure of Brazil was underdeveloped, and depended, both in its civilian and military aspects, on the external supply of technology. The quest for autonomy, however, remained a deep-seated objective of both the civilian and military leaders of the *Estado Nôvo*, which consistently aimed to mobilize the national resources.

In the national mobilization the relationship between private and public economic agents, especially in the military field, is of great significance. In the *Estado Nôvo* the private companies kept financial and organizational control over most of the arms production, while the military supervised its technical aspects (Hilton 1982, pp. 657-62). In other words, a coalition developed in the prewar military production of Brazil between private and public interests in which the state defined the direction and the companies were responsible for implementing the plans.

The military industrialization of Brazil in the 1950s and the 1960s continued the import-substitution model that had been introduced in the 1930s. This model was facilitated by the drive to technological maturity in the 1950s, which was the next step after the regional takeoff had taken place in São Paulo at the beginning of the century and the national takeoff in the 1930s and the 1940s (Rostow 1978, pp. 485-6).

The deep-seated interest of Brazil's military in strengthening the country's arms manufacturing base had been compatible with Vargas's policy in the 1930s and helped him to return to power in 1951-54. Furthermore, the outbreak of World War II enabled and justified the advocacy by military of its interests in the military industrialization (Skidmore 1967, pp. 41-7). The political and military elite did not have confidence in the reliability of leading powers to deliver, in a real crisis, weapons to Brazil. In particular, the Brazilians were frustrated with their dependence on US weapons supplies. In order to reduce that dependence, Brazil diversified its sources of supply from the 1950s onwards and bought arms from various West European countries (Hilton 1982, pp. 665-6; Brigagao 1986, pp. 104-5).

Autonomy and Dependence

The ultimate goal, however, was a greater military-industrial autonomy which was regarded as the key to greater national power and national security. This developmentalist nationalism has been a driving force in the Brazilian economic and military policy at least since the 1930s (Skidmore 1967, pp. 88-9).

Brazil's economic and technological policy since the 1950s has been characterized as pragmatic anti-dependency strategy. It has been pragmatic in advocating the blending of foreign and indigenous technologies to achieve a relationship of selective interdependence with the outside world. Technological self-determination rather than technological self-sufficiency has been the main objective. According to this thinking, the state should prepare science and technology plans to specify objectives and instruments of technology policy, including the code of conduct for the transnational companies operating in the country. The state should make self-determination visible and decide the ground rules for developing indigenous technologies and importing foreign technologies. The corporations, however, should have considerable autonomy in utilizing the technology in the market (Adler 1987, pp. 75-82).

The import-substituting industrialization in Brazil created in the course of the 1950s a diversified capital-goods sector, which is a necessary precondition for arms manufacturing in a semi-peripheral economy. Shipbuilding, the automobile industry and the production of heavy mechanical and electrical equipment expanded strongly under the aegis of the import-substitution policy (Adler 1987, p. 153). All these industries were relevant for the development of arms production, the basis of which was consequently strengthened in the 1950s. Domestic industry was given priority in the procurement policies of the armed forces.

This objective called for the strengthening of military technical expertise by sending officers to receive technical training abroad. This training was usually associated with the acquisition of foreign weapons, but also contributed to indigenous technical knowledge (Hilton 1982, p. 667-8). The domestic organization of military research, development and training was also developed within individual services. The establishment of Instituto Tecnologico de Aeronautica (ITA) and Centro Téchnico da Aeronáutica (CTA), the research and training centre of the air force, in the early 1950s was particularly important as they became the kernel of the civilian and military aircraft industry. In fact, the impact of the CTA, based in São José dos Campos, was diffused to other sectors of the military industry as well (Wöhlcke 1987, pp. 13-15).

The Doctrine of Security and Development

The Escola Superior de Guerra (ESG) was established in 1949 and became a centre for developing the security ideology and setting priorities for the Brazilian military. It was instrumental in developing the doctrine of security and development (*seguranca e desenvolvimiento*). This doctrine has been a part of the Brazilian concept of national power as a comprehensive and indivisible resource of material character (Burgess and Wolff 1979; Arruda 1980).

The doctrine of security and development was further entrenched in Brazilian policy after the military coup in 1964 and especially in 1964-7. It had three central elements: counter-insurgency, integration of the country's peripheries to its central regions, and industrialization as a key to military power (Crow and Thorpe 1988, p. 219). In particular, after 1974 the ESG doctrine changed and it appropriated the critical issues of opposition, participation, non-governmental parties and elections into its agenda. In that way, the ESG helped to neutralize the pressure growing in the civil society against the military government (Stepan 1988, pp. 45-54). The stabilizing function of the ESG doctrine can be seen also in its tendency to favour the participation of private companies in the military production in order to retain the linkages with the civilian industry and to prevent arms manufacturing from becoming a military enclave (Franko-Jones 1988, p. 47).

In this study only one aspect of the national security doctrine, that is, industrialization, is explored. The Brazilian military industry started in most cases as a private endeavour, but, because of a weak infrastructure, lack of technical abilities and other reasons, they largely failed. This failure forced the state to intervene in order to maintain the indigenous ability to turn out weapons (Franko-Jones 1988, pp. 48-50). Thus, new arms manufacturers were established and the old ones were restructured and rationalized in the course of the 1960s and the 1970s. Esepecially after the military coup in 1964 the government of Carlos Castello Branco forged an alliance between the military and the government-subsidized industries in order to mobilize Brazil's industrial resources and its excess capacity for military production.

The Industrialization Mobilization Plan of the military government built on the automobile, electrical and steel industries that were created by the import-substituting policy (Brigagao 1984, pp. 39-41; Brigagao 1986, pp. 105-6). Industrialization in Brazil had a strategic character during the military regime; it was promoted not only for economic, but for national political reasons as well. This is reflected in the emphasis on the development of the domestic capital goods industry, which by the end of the 1970s satisfied about 80 per cent of the national demand. The downside of this success was that the importation of technology and capital increased concomitantly with the expansion of the capital goods industry (Moltmann 1989, pp. 94-6).

The armaments policy was initiated by the export imperative. The export strategy called, in its turn, for government subsidies for the development and production of weapons. These subsidies have co-existed with the commercialization of the Brazilian armaments industry as a result of the expanded role given to private domestic and transnational companies (Brigagao 1986, pp. 106-8).

The state ownership is dominant in the production of small arms and ammunition. In 1975 the government consolidated several small companies, which had previously produced small arms under individual services, into a bigger industrial unit known as Empresa Brasileira de Material Bélico (IMBEL). The chief functions of this holding company has been to integrate the previously independent companies, to increase investment in the small-arms industry and to commercialize their exports and imports. In the early 1980s the military relaxed its control of IMBEL, which has now a mixed state-private ownership. IMBEL has favoured the participation of foreign companies in its operation provided that they bring capital and technology with them (Brigagao 1984, pp. 44-7 and Brigagao 1986, p. 108).

In the aerospace sector the co-operation between the Brazilian state and private companies is most intense. The mixture of ownership assures that the companies receive subsidies and protection from the state, while, at the same time, they are in a position to benefit from the operation of the commercial market. The story of the Brazilian aircraft industry suggests that the statist and market aspects of the military-industrial complex should be integrated in the same analytical framework.

The private-public co-operation in the Brazilian arms industry is typical of late-industrializing countries which aspire to climb up in the international economic hierarchy. The participation of the state is needed because of the extensive capital needs of the new industries. "Thus the state will tend to mobilize funds and create or organise larger productive units which have greater economies of scale". The requirements of international military-industrial rivalry means that arms industries are state-owned and are more protected than most others (Gill and Law 1988, pp. 103-4). The stress on the role of the state is justified, but the authors may go too far in that respect and neglect the critical role of private companies and the private-public symbiosis in the arms economies of late-industrializing countries.

The Arms Manufacturers

São José de Campos is the centre of the Brazilian aircraft industry. The organizations, Embraer, Engesa and Avibras, having between them in the early 1980s a total of nearly 14,000 employees, are all located there. São José de Campos is a prototype of private-public co-operation. The government has constructed the necessary infrastructure there, and maintains extensive R&D and training facilities underpinning the economic dynamism of this "industrial park", unique in Brazil (Lock 1986, p. 84).

Empresa Brasileira de Aeronáutica (Embraer) was established in 1969 to produce both civilian and military aircraft. In the civilian market EMB-110 Banderainte has become a success story and it has been purchased by several airlines of industrialized countries. Embraer is now more than 90 per cent owned by private shareholders, but its R&D expenses, for instance, are partially funded by the state through the CTA. In fact, through the CTA the Brazilian state has tailored a supportive technology policy for Embraer, but has left its hands largely free in production and marketing (Franko-Jones 1988, p. 56). Embraer has in Brazil a network of some 300 subcontractors, among them a wholly-owned subsidiary, Neiva, in São Paulo.

In 1971 Embraer started to develop, under a licence from Aeronautica Macchi, a trainer version of EMB-326 Xavante. In 1980 the prototype of the EMB-312 Tucano trainer was flown. In 1985 Embraer concluded a deal for production under licence by Short Brothers in Belfast of 130 Tucanos for the British Royal Air Force as their new basic trainer. Egypt is also producing Tucanos and some 30 developing countries have purchased it. The most ambitious project of Embraer is the AMX tactical fighter which it jointly develops with Aermacchi and Aeritalia. It is expected to compete in the export markets with the ageing Migs and A-4 Skyhawks.

Embraer is a good example of the policy of pragmatic anti-dependence. It pursues rather extensive R&D activities and controls the production of military hardware. Yet, Embraer has to admit that it is unable to source all the necessary components and technologies from the home market and, as a consequence, it has to resort to imports. Estimates vary, but it is usually pointed out that Embraer has to import about 60 per cent of the components it needs. Embraer deliberately aims to expand its indigenous capacity, though initially in co-operation with transnational arms manufacturers. A recent example is the co-operation agreement concluded between Embraer and Sikorsky Aircraft for the manufacturing in Brazil of composite materials for aircraft production.

The share of imported components is higher in the aircraft industry than in the production of, for example, military vehicles and artillery. The reason is simply that the aircraft industry is technologically more demanding and the need for foreign supplies usually concerns the most complex components. Foreign dependence is most visible in the production of aircraft engines where co-operation with Pratt & Whitney has been of pivotal importance for the Brazilian aircraft industry.

The most important foreign partners of technological co-operation have been Piper and Aermacchi. Piper has collaborated with Embraer mainly in the development and production of business aircraft for the domestic and, to a lesser extent, international market. Embraer has also done subcontracting for the international production network of Piper. Their co-operation has been a two-way project, but characterized by asymmetries in the technological capabilities of the partners. Aermacchi and Aeritalia have co-operated with Embraer in the development and production of the MB-326 Xavante and the AMX military aircraft. In addition, several other transnational corporations, such as Northrop, Lockheed and Fokker, have been involved in the Brazilian aircraft industry.

Another major military contractor located at São José dos Campos is Engesa (Engenheiros Especializados) which was established in 1960 to produce equipment for the oil-drilling industry. It is a privately-owned concern employing 10,000 people and comprising six industrial production divisions and a number of service divisions such as Engesa Viaturas, Engex, Engequimica, Engesa FNV and Engetrônica. These divisions produce, among other things, armoured vehicles, guns and ammunition, military electronics and related civilian applications. Engesa is heavily specialized in the military market: 95 per cent of its production is for military purposes and some 60 per cent of it is for export. Engexco, the trading company of Engesa, is responsible for the international marketing of military and civilian products.

Although Engesa is a private company, it is supported by the government with low-interest loans and R&D subsidies. Engesa is especially known for its production of military vehicles, including Urutu, Cascavel, Jararaca and Sucuri wheeled armoured personnel carriers in which it is the biggest producer in the world. The carriers are based on domestic design, although the engines have been produced by Mercedes Benz Brasil. Engesa's military vehicles have been exported to over 20 Third World countries, including Iraq and Libya, in addition to several Latin American countries. A main reason for the demand for Engesa's armoured vehicles is their durability and operability in the rugged local conditions.

Engesa's latest project is the tracked Osorio main battle tank which was started in 1983. The Osorio tank is built both for the Brazilian army and for export; orders are expected from Libya'and Saudi Arabia. Engesa has been hopeful in receiving a $2 billion contract for these tanks from Saudi Arabia, but the order has been dependent on financial arrangements. Engesa is developing two different versions of the Osario in order to be able to compete more effectively with the other comparable tanks available in the international market. The ultimate aim of Engesa is to develop an entire family of battle tanks based on the Osario chassis.

In early 1990 it became clear that both Avibras and Engesa were in deep economic trouble and faced the danger of bankruptcy. The main reason for their difficulties was the decline in arms orders in the Middle East, which the Brazilian manufacturers have extensively supplied. Avibras has been estimated to have transferred weapons worth $1 billion to the Persian Gulf, in particular to Iraq during its war with Iran (*Business Week*, 16 April 1990, p. 23; Cochran and Ward 1991, p. 21). In general, the decline of arms exports has badly hurt the Brazilian arms industry. In addition, its state-owned component has faced uncertainties because of the privatization policy of the new government.

Engesa's problems are, in part, due to the excessive development costs of the Osorio battle tank and the uncertainties concerning the Saudi order. A typical pattern of Brazil's arms industry emerged as a result of Engesa's difficulties. In co-operation with Embraer and Engesa, the military arranged a new company, Orbita, to produce medium-range missiles, and prompted Engesa to team up with Aerospatiale to produce helicopters for the Brazilian navy. These supportive measures are intended to assure the continuity of arms manufacturing in the middle of internal and external pressures (Franko-Jones 1988, pp. 61-2).

Avibras Aeroespacial is a private company, established in 1962. It develops and produces missiles both for civilian and military uses, ranging from artillery rockets to air-to-surface missiles. Since the early Sonda sounding rockets, Avibras has actively participated in Brazil's ambitious space programme. Located in São José dos Campos it has three semi-independent subsidiaries - Tectran, Tectronic and Transvip - which specialize in vehicles and electronics both for military and civilian applications. Avibras has 4,000 employees.

Like other private arms manufacturers, Avibras also co-operates with the state-run research and training centres, in particular with CTA. This centre is also involved in the production of missiles (Roland and Cobra under licences from MBB and Aérospatiale). Aérospatiale is also a co-owner, together with the state of Minais Gerais, of Helibras (Helicopteros do Brasil). Helibras, established in 1980, is located in Itajubá, Minais Gerais. The company has been geared to co-produce French helicopters for the

Brazilian military and for exports. Although production has started and small orders have been placed by Bolivia and Chile, Helibras appears to having difficulties in progressing to a sustained development and production of helicopters.

One of Avibras's key projects has been Astros (Artillery Saturation Rocket System) with the range of 40 to 70 kilometres. The fire-control system of Astros was purchased from a Swiss company, Contravenes. The follow-up model, Astros II, has been exported to Iraq, Libya and Saudi Arabia.

The success of Embraer, Engesa and other companies has encouraged a considerable number of medium-sized companies to enter the military market. They have been established on top of traditional arms manufacturers such as Companhia de Explosivos Valparaiba and Companhia Brasileira de Cartuchos (CBC). The latter organization was established in 1926 as a private domestic company, but was taken over in the 1930s by Remington and Imperial Chemical Industries. Since 1980 it has been 30 per cent owned by IMBEL and 70 per cent privately owned. CBC produces primarily firearms and ammunition, of which some two-thirds is exported to more than 65 countries.

Companhia Brasileira de Cartuchos is located in a São Paulo suburb. In general, São Paulo is the centre of privately-owned arms manufacturers such as Bernardini (modernization and construction of tanks), Taurus SA (small arms and communication systems), D.F. Vasconcellos SA (optics and antitank weapons) and Moto Pecas SA (military vehicles and their components). Privately-owned D.F. Vasconcellos specializes in genuine high-tech and produces advanced optronic equipment.

Many São Paulo companies have co-operated closely with the Army's Technology Centre (Centro Technológico do Exercito, CETEX), which was established in 1979 to invest in human resources, informatics, testing and subsidiary industries. The idea has been, as in CTA, to produce technology and relevant expertise without commercializing it; this task has been left to the arms manufacturers themselves (Franko-Jones 1988, pp. 56-7). With CETEX's support Bernardini developed for the army a new battle tank, the MB-3 Tamyo, and now plans a complete family of Tamyo tanks. In 1982, CETEX awarded to Moto Pecas a contract for the modernization of the M-113 armoured personnel carrier to function mainly as C3 vehicles. Moto Pecas has co-operated in technology with Saab Scania and with the Brazilian subsidiaries of AEG and Philips.

A pertinent feature of some of these São Paulo companies, in particular Taurus and CBC, is that they were in foreign ownership but in the late 1970s were bought back by Brazilian interests. Until 1975 the main shareholder of Taurus was Smith & Wesson which exported the products of its Brazilian partner to other Latin American countries. Since the Brazilian takeover of Taurus, its exports to Latin America have continued and expanded considerably to the United States. As a consequence, Taurus International Manufacturing was established in Miami to produce firearms for the local market. Bernardini exports 20 per cent and Taurus 40 per cent of its products.

Historically, the naval construction has been the least indigenous branch of the Brazilian military industry. The needs of the navy have been met either by imports or the licenced production of foreign vessels. The big exception is the state-owned Arsenal da Marinha do Rio de Janeiro (AMRJ). It was established in 1763 and is, with its 7,000 employees, the biggest shipyard in Brazil. It has built destroyers, corvettes and other ships and has exported a river patrol boat to Paraguay (thus, in comparison to Embraer and Engesa, its export performance has been quite modest).

Another major dockyard is Verolme Estaleiros Reunidos do Brasil SA which was launched in the late 1950s as a co-operative venture between the Brazilian state and a Dutch company, Cornelis Verolme. Later, the company, located in the state of Rio de Janeiro, was taken over by private Brazilian capital. Verolme has participated in a new company, Cenabra, which was established to develop and produce an indigenous corvette, called the Inhauma class. The Inhauma may be becoming an economic disaster, which has prompted Verolme to diversify away from the military business.

Ishibras-Ishikawajima do Brasil is 90 per cent owned by Ishikawajima-Harima Heavy Industries of Japan. The company, also located in the state of Rio de Janeiro, has been constructing for the Brazilian Navy since the late 1960s. Ishibras-Ishikawajima is in reality an industrial and commercial group which is primarily active in non-military areas. In Brazil, there are also some new companies that are making efforts to conclude development and production contracts with the Brazilian Navy; they include FI Indústria e Comércio and Industrias Reunidas Caneco (Kapstein 1990, p. 590; Wöhlcke 1987, pp. 15-27, 130-52; Evans 1986, p. 106-8; Lock 1986; Revuelta 1985; Brigagao 1985, pp. 59-68; Tuomi and Väyrynen 1982, pp. 150-3; Perry 1978, pp. 17-22).

Military Industry: A National Objective

Several factors stand out in the organization and operation of Brazil's arms industry. Its establishment was motivated by long-term political objectives. Arms production was started to reduce Brazil's dependence on foreign suppliers of weapons who, it was feared, might be unreliable in times of crises. Military capacity was also acquired to cope with the internal problems of the country and to expand its regional hegemony (Kapstein 1990, pp. 582-4). However, it soon became clear that a self-contained arms industry was not feasible in a country whose economic structure was polarized and whose technology was underdeveloped.

The Brazilian authorities realized the basic problem and developed a strategy to deal with it. In the short term, advanced components of military technology were imported and absorbed into the domestic industry. In order to recover some of the expenses caused by the technology imports, the export drive on weapons was initiated. Thus, arms manufacturing in Brazil, once it was seriously launched in the 1960s, had to be inserted into the global network of arms production and exports.

In general, the Brazilian military government deliberately welcomed transnational corporations (TNCs) during the years of heady economic growth in the late 1960s and early 1970s. According to a popular interpretation, a coalition of the state, international business and national bourgeoisie developed in Brazil at that stage have co-operated closely with the Army's Technology Centre (Centro Technol 1954).

The Brazilian government has welcomed the direct investment and technology transfers by the TNCs. In some priority areas, such as capital goods, raw materials and mining, preference has, however, been given to Brazilian enterprises. Although transnational corporations have been permitted to establish wholly-owned subsidiaries, the Brazilian government has given precedence to joint ventures. Occasionally, foreign partners, instead of going it alone, have been almost forced to co-operate with local companies. This has been particularly true in the military industry in which wholly-owned subsidiaries of the TNCs are a rare phenomenon and joint ventures with US and, increasingly, West European companies are much more common. Obviously, joint ventures are favoured by the Brazilians as their activities are easier to steer and they provide an opportunity to share foreign technology. Control over the partner and access to technology can be more easily exercised in joint ventures than in wholly-owned subsidiaries (Brigagao 1985, pp. 46-7).

The foreign control of Brazil's military industry by direct investment is very limited. The arms economy is organized by product groups - which largely eliminates competition. If foreign companies want to enter Brazil's military market they have to comply with the market-sharing arrangements of the host companies (Wöhlcke 1987, p. 37). As transnational corporations have been tied to the local networks of power, they have contributed in several ways to the rise of Brazil's military industry.

An important contribution is the role of TNCs in strengthening the country's manufacturing potential, especially in the transportation and machinery industries. Without such capital-goods industries there cannot be any significant military production either. In the beginning, the technological input of foreign companies was geared to the civilian market, but the military system of Brazil made extensive use of the dual-use character of technology in automotive and machinery industries (Evans 1986, p. 105; Revuelta 1985, p. 92). It is no accident that the private and semi-private arms industry is concentrated in the state of São Paolo which is Brazil's industrial heartland. Its industrial revolution provided a backdrop for the development of the military industry as well.

The liberal delivery of vehicle components, engines, electronics and special metals by the TNC subsidiaries to Brazil's military industry propped up its development and production efforts. A further advantage of the TNC technology was that its components are internationally standardized. This has helped to maintain and repair the Brazilian military aircraft and armoured vehicles in a wide variety of circumstances abroad (Brzoska 1987, pp. 12-13). The lack of domestic alternatives and the promise of global operations pushed the military government of Brazil to acquire advanced technology.

For this purpose, the government established science and technology centres and policies to guide the development and assimilation of technologies by plans, controls and incentives. The government also actively purchased foreign technology to blend it with indigenous capabilities and to create a sound basis for domestic manufacturing. To achieve this objective, the government was ready to shoulder short-term costs to harvest expected long-term benefits. That is why production under licence and co-production were preferred as they gave a chance to train the local workforce, indigenize components and conclude co-operative relations with TNCs.

In a word, the establishment of selective interdependence in technology has been the hallmark of the government's policy in Brazil. A concrete example of this approach is the agreement concluded by the AMRJ in 1970 to build, in co-operation with the British Vosper Thornycroft, six Niteroi class frigates, although it would have been cheaper to buy them outright. Some of the Brazilian workforce participated in the construction of the first frigates in Britain and in this way became acquainted with the technology. Subsequently, British experts went to Brazil to continue to co-operate in the construction of the remaining frigates (Lock 1986, pp. 95-6).

The continued need for British expertise shows that the indigenization of naval technology has either faced serious obstacles or has not been tried seriously. Michel Brzoska combines these two interpretations: "The Navy has not cooperated in the joint armed forces/private industry drive for military industrialization and demands more sophisticated weapons that can only be produced with much foreign support" (Brzoska 1987, p. 13). As a result, the navy has been unwilling to become deeply involved in naval construction. Instead, it has been more interested in developing explosives, electronics and guidance systems to be used in the vessels. In effect, the navy has made considerable technological progress and kept TNCs at bay in these lucrative areas (Barros 1984, p. 82; Tuomi and Väyrynen 1982, pp. 153-4).

As hinted by Brzoska, the army has been the leading force behind the military industrialization of Brazil. It has established R&D centres and otherwise supported the technological modernization of old weapons systems and the development of new ones, with the help of foreign companies if needed (Brigagao 1984, pp. 64-6). The technological interest of the army has made Brazil self-sufficient in small arms and ammunition and has created for the country a flourishing military vehicles industry. Similarly, the air force has promoted, both institutionally and financially, the development of new weapons, their components and materials (Brigagao 1984, pp. 59-61).

The state is an important factor in the Brazilian arms industry; it purchases weapons, protects and subsidizes domestic production, organizes training and research, and steers arms exports. Indeed, in Brazil's arms production and arms exports the state is a multifunctional actor. Within the state apparatus the military has developed various institutional mechanisms by which it is able to benefit from the expansion of the arms industry (Wöhlcke 1987, pp. 38-43). In other words, there is a close relationship and vested interests between the army and the state machinery. The role of the Brazilian army in the military industry is but one example of the military prerogatives which have emerged since the 1930s (Stepan 1988, pp. 103-14).

Yet it is worth keeping in mind that in all the product groups of the Brazilian arms industry there is a strong private presence and, in reality, its importance is decisive. This point is supported by Carol Evans (1986, p. 104) who observes that "the military was a factor *facilitating* rather than *determining* the development of Brazilian arms production" (emphasis in the original). In Brazilian arms manufacturing private companies, both national and transnational, have apparently fostered economic dynamism and technological advance. In effect, the encouragement of private arms production has been intended to create a more dynamic, diversified and qualified military industry (Wöhlcke 1987, pp. 36-7). However, the private contribution has been underwritten by the state and the military, which have supported the military industry both directly and indirectly.

Although private capital is largely running the Brazilian arms industry, the present system of development, production and marketing could not have emerged without the support of the state. At the very least, the state has had the role of an initiator; it has launched production in new areas which have subsequently been taken over by the private domestic companies. This is a typical course of action in import-substituting industrialization. In the Brazilian arms industry the state has been both an "entrepreneur" and a "landlord".

In Brazil, the arms industry has systematically exploited the dual-use technologies to increase its level of qualification. An example of the spill-over effect is the impact of the motor industry on the production of military vehicles. The motor industry has been one of the keystones in the Brazilian *milagre econômico* as, together with metallurgy, mechanical engineering and the electrical industry, it formed its integrated leading sector. In particular, Volkswagen's automotive technology was adopted to manufacture military vehicles (Evans 1986, p. 105; Crow and Thorpe 1988, p. 228). Volkswagen Brazil is also one of the private shareholders of Embraer. In addition, the Swedish company Scania has turned out engines for tanks and military vehicles (Wöhlcke 1987, pp. 40-1).

The deliberate pursuit by Brazil of technological sophistication has had its costs as well. The domestic expansion of the capital goods industry has been associated with the transnationalization of the system of import-substituting industrialization. It has been accompanied, however, by a chronic deficit in the current account, which has three main causes: the escalation of upper-class and middle-class consumption; the 1973 and 1979 hikes in oil prices; and the import-intensity of the industrialization model.

The imbalance in the current account has been crystallized in the motor industry whose "balance of payments contribution . . . was decidedly negative throughout the miracle period". The negative effect was caused largely by the increase in oil prices, but also by the extensive imports of capital goods by the motor industry (Crow and Thorpe 1988, pp. 233-4; Skidmore 1988, pp. 139-40). In effect, import substitution increases rather than decreases import requirements. Moreover, import substitution "tends to raise the costs of imports as it becomes necessary to import ever more technically complicated, advanced, monopolized, and thus costly equipment from the metropolis (Frank 1969; 234-35).

The high-growth and technology-intensive economic strategy of the military government was sustained by the continued inflow of borrowed money. Towards the end of the 1970s the balance-of-payment problem started to become serious as hope waned that exports would produce sufficient earnings to service the debt. The debt-led growth came to a stalemate at the beginning of the 1980s when the Brazilian economy entered a period of depression from which it has been only slowly recovering. During the depression, the imports, in particular those of capital goods, were slashed down in order to save foreign exchange. In that way the depression cut directly into the heart of Brazil's industrial strategy. The gradual recovery of the Brazilian economy has been significantly aided by the strong performance of exports since the depression period (Skidmore 1988, pp. 178-80, 206-9, 230-40 and 254-55).

Arms Exports

The Brazilian armaments economy is export-oriented, and not accidentally but because of deliberate government policy. Programa Nacional de Exportacao de Material Bélico (PNEMEM) stimulates and directs the arms exports. Their production by the government reflects the role of expanding arms deliveries in the strengthening of the military industrial basis of Brazilian "nation empire" and its international connections (Brigagao 1984, pp. 28-30). Yet Brazilian arms exports, though built on political foundations, are not restricted by political considerations. In fact, "the major contribution of the Brazilian government has been to do nothing" (Franko-Jones 1988, p. 59; see also Kapstein 1990, p. 585).

There has also been an economic element in Brazil's arms exports. As the costs of developing and importing technological inputs to weapons systems have been soaring, the need to export has increased. The sale of weapons, for example, fighters and missiles, has taken place in an increasingly competitive market. On that basis it is justified to suggest that the growth of Brazilian arms exports is stagnating, and instead of moving almost in a linear manner to increasingly higher levels of technological sophistication, the sales items may belong to lower-tech categories (Kapstein 1990, pp. 591-2).

In 1980-4, Brazil's share of the total Third World production of major weapons was about 10 per cent, while its exports accounted for 23 per cent of the Third World total. The export share of the total arms production has been high, about two-thirds. Nearly one-half of the Brazilian arms exports went to the Middle East, in particular Iraq (*World Armaments* 1987, p. 198). The export drive of Brazil's military industry is, however, of rather recent origin; until the 1970s exports were limited, and only then started to expand. According to one estimate the Brazilian arms exports amounted to almost $1 billion per year in the early 1980s, accounting for 4 to 5 per cent of the total exports (Brzoska and Ohlson 1986, pp. 114-15).

The $1 billion figure is at variance with another SIPRI estimate which informs us that at constant 1985 prices Brazil's arms exports varied in 1976-9 between $100-150 million, jumped to about 250 million in 1980-4, declined to about $150 million in 1985-6, and escalated to $466 and $338 million in 1987 and 1988 respectively (*World Armaments* 1989, pp. 228-9). The decrease of Brazil's arms exports in 1985-6 was consistent with the overall decline in the global arms trade caused by the growing indebtedness and the decrease in oil prices. The increase in 1987-8 is more difficult to explain, but it was obviously related to the extensive delivery of weapons to the Persian Gulf. In any case, about 90 per cent of Brazil's exports of major weapons have gone to other Third World countries (*World Armaments* 1989, pp. 198-9).

Although arms exports have earned foreign exchange for Brazil, the income has been modest in comparison with Brazil's external debt and the costs to service it. A direct comparison of the value of imports and exports of major weapons by Brazil provides a positive balance sheet in the 1980s. This has been due in part to the overall decline of imports as a result of the economic depression (Brzoska and Ohlson 1986, p. 32). Such mechanical comparison, however, does not take into account the value of capital goods and other imported inputs that are needed in the production of arms. A detailed scrutiny of the export and import patterns of the Brazilian aeronautical industry in the 1970s and the early 1980s suggests that the imports of various components clearly exceeded the value of Embraer's export (Lock 1986, pp. 86-7; Kapstein 1990, p. 589).

Since then the situation may have changed somewhat, but the fact remains that the Brazilian arms industry is not propped up principally because of its capacity to earn foreign exchange. Rather the non-restrictive export policy of weapons is a consequence of the decision to develop in Brazil an autonomous, high-technology armaments industry. The underlying decision is politically motivated and state-oriented. The state-orientation is also reflected in Brazil's determination to sell only to other governments and in no circumstances to opposition movements and other non-government groups.

The political commitment of the Brazilian government to develop a strong arms industry helps to understand that its "defense industry has not experienced the constraints that most civilian industrial sectors faced and continue to face due to economic recession and government austerity policies" (Brigagao 1986, p. 111). There is, however, some evidence that the economic depression also curtailed the privileges of the military. This is evidenced by the development of Brazil's military spending. Since 1982 there has been no real increase in military expenditure, except for a small peak in 1986 and a decline in 1987; it has stayed at about $1.8-2.0 billion, at constant 1986 prices. Because of the decline in Brazil's GNP over most of the 1980s the share allotted to military spending has not dropped in any drastic manner, but has stayed at 0.8-0.9 per cent (*World Armaments* 1989, pp. 187, 192).

Military Technology and Development

The lessons to be learned from the Brazilian experience are mixed. To my mind, it is beyond doubt that the semi-peripheral industrial revolution in Brazil has underpinned the growth of military industry, which has been, in the first place, politically motivated. It has been Brazil's political religion that full-fledged national greatness requires, in addition to geographic and demographic size, a strong and advanced industrial sector that creates a self-sustaining domestic economy and is competitive in the international export market. The industrial strength lends it hand to the military by providing the tools of its profession through which domestic stability and international prestige can be assured.

Industrial development benefits arms manufacturing, but does the reverse relationship exist? It is often suggested that domestic development and foreign acquisition of advanced military industry injects dynamism into the industry, provides qualified jobs and saves foreign exchanged by import substitution. Empirical studies suggest that the overall effect of military spending on Brazil's economy has been positive (Cochran and Ward 1991, pp. 22-8). All these arguments have a degree of validity in Brazil, but should at the same time be treated with caution. As in any other country, weapons systems do not feed back into the economic processes as their civilian counterparts would do; also, alternative allocation of resources would create more jobs than the military industry, and the savings in foreign exchange are undermined by the costs of imported intermediary inputs (Wöhlcke 1987, pp. 89-92).

Yet the argument can be put forward that in Brazil there are special factors that have made the spill-over effect from the military to the civilian industry more tangible than in most other Third World arms manufacturers. The main factor is perhaps the compatibility of the military and civilian industrial endowments (Brzoska 1987, p. 20). Their technological sophistication and skill levels are not far removed - as is the case, for example, in India - but support each other in a mutually beneficial manner.

Furthermore, the civilian and military industries are linked with each other. The state-directed acquisition of technology helps to extract from foreign suppliers and their subsidiaries in Brazil inputs that might not otherwise have been available. These inputs are also readily integrated into the domestic industrial process and specifically into its indigenization. This is possible for at least two reasons: the military extensively sponsors R&D, laying the basis for the indigenization of technology; and the participation of private industry in arms manufacturing helps to avoid bureaucratic inertia. Thus the "public-private partnership" breaks down the military-civilian divide and allows the civilian industry to benefit from the public money allocated for arms production (Franko-Jones 1988).

The military R&D centres such as Centro Technológico do Exército (CETEX), Centro Téchnico Aeroespacial (CTA), Centro de Pesquisas da Marinha (CPM), Instituto Militar de Engenharia (IME) and others have significantly contributed to the development of military technology and technical skills. These centres are not separate research institutions, but are closely integrated both with the government's industrial and technology policy and with private industry. They are sponsored by Grupo Permanente de Mobilizacao Industrial (GPMI), a group established in 1965 by private São Paulo industrialists to integrate civilian and military industries (Brigagao 1984, pp. 39-41; Brigagao 1985; 41-3).

In Brazil, the state co-operates closely with private companies, both national and transnational ones, in the development and production of arms. The mixture of state and private interests varies from one branch of military production to another, but the co-operative pattern prevails in all of them (Lock 1986, p. 100). This state-private mixture, in which the state supports and steers and the private companies perform, appears to be an important explanation for the success of Brazil's arms industry. In Brazil, the "economy has been a mixture of market mechanism, state intervention and planning; the productive sector has combined private (domestic and foreign) and state enterprises. The state has played an important economic role through guidelines and planning, incentives and controls - establishing the objectives and the means to achieve progress" (Adler 1987, p. 186). On the other hand, the role of private industry makes that an extreme case for the strategic origins of industrialization and the spill-over effect is not supported by the Brazilian case.

The Brazilian experience lends support to the hypothesis that in an upwardly mobile semi-peripheral country military industry can also stimulate civilian industrial development. This presupposes, however, that the military industry is properly organized, its technological sophistication is adjusted to the local circumstances, and dual-use technologies are systematically exploited. On the other hand, it is quite clear that an alternative investment of financial, technical and human resources in civilian industry would have produced better results in terms of socially equitable economic development. In that regard, Brazil's performance leaves much to be desired (Wöhlcke 1987, pp. 103-12).

The pivotal question may not be whether military industry has supported civilian economic development or not, but whether there is any genuine alternative to the present Brazilian model of development. There is political space for an alternative since there is no serious security threat in Brazil's neighbourhood; it could further cut back its military spending, although it is already low by the standards of major powers, without jeopardizing its security. However, there are other constraints that make any alternative model rather unlikely in the Brazilian case.

Brazil is a semi-peripheral country in which the national elite has anchored itself in a dual strategy comprising, first, the internal colonization and consolidation of the vast territory, and secondly, the strengthening of its role as the regional and, ultimately, the global power centre. The domestic and international policy of the ruling elite in Brazil is built on a geopolitical scheme which remains quite stable from one type of regime to another. This scheme is associated with "pragmatic antidependency" (Adler 1987) in the economic and technological policy which strives to increase the autonomy of the nation's infrastructure. Such an autonomy, which concerns also military industrialization, is an important precondition for the consolidation of the Brazilian dominance in the Western hemisphere.

As Brazil appears to be chained to the present economic and political strategy, there are only scant possibilities to scale down the military R&D, production and export capabilities. In these circumstances Brazil has developed its military industries in a manner that has not created an excessive burden on the overall process of industrialization. Military industrialization has not been an enemy of the civilian industry, and has, to a degree, supported its development. Yet neither civilian nor military industrialization has been able to solve the persistent poverty and underdevelopment in the country.

Chapter 6
Conclusions

The four case studies carried out above show that the relationship between military industrialization and economic development is necessarily complex, historically variable and dependent on the prevailing international context. That is why there is no universally valid answer to the politically perennial question of whether military spending and industrialization, ultimately, promote or prevent economic development. Any answer has to contain several caveats and qualifications concerning the conditions in which specific relationships between military allocations and economic performance exist.

This does not mean, however, that one is bound to live in uncertainty and accept whatever economic and social effects are generated by military spending. On the contrary, information about the specific relationships between military industry and the economy helps to develop and structure military production in a manner that it produces as little economic damage as possible and even yields economic benefits. Bradley T. Shaw (1987) has shown that the overlapping region of military and civilian technologies experience faster than average development. While it is a fact that military criteria shape the development of technology towards large and centralized systems, these criteria can be bent to comply to civilian needs as well. It appears that the military and civilian industries are better integrated in market economies, while they are separated by organizational barriers in planned economies (Schomacker, Wilke and Wulf 1987, pp. 63-4).

In general, in structuring the arms industry military technical requirements should not attract too much attention but, at the same time, their civilian economic effects should be carefully monitored and assessed. The maxim could be that in the absence of an economically viable and appropriate structure, the military industry would have counter-productive effects and, in the long run, would weaken the national security it is supposed to serve. Left on its own, the arms industry would not only build up the arms race, but would also produce structural dislocations in the economy.

The basic findings of the study vary from one country to another. In the rising powers, that is, Japan and Brazil, there is a degree of positive interaction between military industrialization and economic development. Their experiences conform with the general observation made by A.F. Mullins, on the basis of a cross-national statistical survey, that trends in national military capabilities depend on GNP growth: "capability rises after several good years of GNP growth and then levels off after GNP stagnates or declines". In other words, the expansion of economic capabilities permits the accumulation of military power, which may, however, undermine the prospects for economic growth over the long term (Mullins 1987, pp. 106-7).

The establishment of a sufficient capital-goods industry is a necessary precondition for arms manufacturing capacity and prevents the emergence of a too lopsided and dualistic economic structure. The causal relationship is very clear here: industrialization, and, in particular, heavy industrialization, permits the development of arms production if there is a political decision to embark on it. From this perspective it is no wonder that both Japan and Brazil invested extensively in the establishment of a domestic iron and steel industry in order to avoid the dependence on imports in this strategically vital sector. The steel industry, in turn, has been integrated with shipbuilding and the production of military vehicles.

Once established the arms industry is not a neutral agent in the economy. It often spreads new production processes and standards, encourages R&D-intensive activities and favours new management practices. That is why it is misleading to explore the impact of military production only in terms of its ability to generate new technologies that are potentially applicable also in the civilian economy. In addition, arms production affects the entire society: "the significance of military enterprise can be appreciated only within the larger social and institutional context" (Smith 1987, p. 21). As suggested in the opening chapter the compatibility of agents, organization and technologies is an important factor in creating technological paradigms and cultures in which the military industry operates.

Especially in Meiji Japan the military industry had created a technological paradigm that pervaded the entire society by spreading modern industrial practices. This dissemination process was closely linked with the policy of importing selectively foreign technology and utilizing foreign experts who fostered economic and social change in Japan. In Brazil, arms production was based until the 1960s on import substitution which was influenced by an anti-dependency attitude. This did not exclude, however, the importation of foreign knowledge and technology. Rather, the search for autonomy through the allocation of resources to domestic R&D and import substitution was intended to internalize the technological element of the arms manufacturing for which Brazil was at that stage dependent on foreign sources.

Indeed, Japan and Brazil are alike in their effort to internalize technology and expertise as a vital ingredient of the national industrial structure. This policy was probably more consistent and hence more efficient in Japan than in Brazil, as reflected in the greater positive contribution of arms manufacturing to Japan's economic development. Especially from the middle of the 1890s onwards, economic growth and military production expanded hand in hand and created a political-industrial juggernaut which was geared to external economic and military expansion *vis-à-vis* its neighbours.

The differences in Japanese and Brazilian experiences may be explained by the differing national motives of their political and military establishments. In Japan, the expansion of military production was closely associated with the country's quest for regional dominance in East Asia and, ultimately, for a global great-power status. The development of an indigenous arms industry was an integral part of Japan's ambitious and expansionist policy. From the days of the Sino-Japanese war in 1895, military expansionism started to feed back to the enlargement of the military industries and, in that way, indirectly to the overall economic development as well.

In Brazil, the level of militarization has been relatively low and, in spite of the doctrine of security and development, military industrialization has not been explicitly connected with expansionist designs beyond its borders. True, the military factor has been relevant in Brazil's institutional and geopolitical consolidation, but it has operated more inside the country and its external dimensions have been primarily political by character. The Brazilian arms industry has also been geared to export, because of the need to recover the costs of import substitution and to earn foreign exchange. In Meiji Japan arms exports were a negligible factor.

An important phenomenon in the establishment and development of arms industries is the intervention of the state in this process. Without the active participation of the state in laying the foundations and funding the nascent industry its growth in a latecomer economy would not be possible. After all, the connection between weapons production and national security makes the role of the state natural in this area. It has been particularly important in financing the development of arms in the public R&D agencies, and this has acted as a kind of subsidy to the private sector. Of course, the state has also funded production, but there has been a tendency gradually to switch it to the private companies. One of the reasons for this policy has been the heavy burden of military production on public finances. In fact, both in Japan and Brazil expanding military expenditures contributed to severe budget crises.

The state involvement in the development and production of arms operates under a cross-pressure. On the one hand, neither in Japan nor in Brazil did the state relinquish its responsibilities even after part of the production was transferred to privately-owned companies. On the other hand, it has been recognized that the state should not become too entrenched in the arms industry. If the industry is entirely state-controlled, there is a double danger of petrification in its structure and the erection of barriers to the transfer of technology and knowledge to the civilian economy. Both in Japan and Brazil there was a blend of public and private interests in the manufacturing of arms. In fact, the state actively sought for the private partnership to share the financial burden and to assure the operation of the spin-off process. It can be argued that this public-private linkage in the arms industry has been in both of these countries a pivotal arrangement to strengthen the positive, albeit limited, contribution of military industry to the overall process of industrialization. This suggests that its structural effects, to use Kahler's terminology, of military spending, can be more significant from the standpoint of economic development than its fiscal effects (Kahler 1988, p. 421).

In the opening chapter a set of hypotheses was developed on the relationship between the international economic context and the nation's international standing on the one hand, and the interaction between military allocations and economic development on the other. The Japanese and Brazilian cases support, although not very conclusively, the idea that in the upwardly mobile countries military industry can make a positive contribution to economic development if its relations with the civilian economy are properly arranged. In other words, the operation of spin-off effects cannot be taken for granted - especially not in regimented societies - but have to be institutionalized by a deliberate policy.

The other hypothesis on the impact of long cycles on the linkage between military and civilian industrialization also receives empirical support. In Japan, the military industry expanded most rapidly during the upswing of the long cycle from the middle of the 1890s to World War I. During this period also the military-civilian linkages intensified and propped up new civilian sectors and enterprises. The Brazilian case study focuses primarily on the downswing period of the long wave from the late 1960s to the present. The contraction in the world economy helps to account for the relatively weaker contribution of military industry to economic development. The effects of contraction are visible, for instance, in the budget problems of the Brazilian state, its burgeoning indebtedness, and the difficulties faced by its export-led strategy of military industrialization. In an expanding world economy, the Brazilian military industry would have probably performed better as measured by macro-economic yardsticks.

A basic point of departure in this study has been the assumption that in downwardly mobile countries the military industry becomes a burden. It not only consumes scarce financial and skilled human resources, but also creates political and bureaucratic obstacles to the restructuring of the industrial system in general. In that way it may even accelerate the downward trend in a nation's economic career. Again, a technological paradigm of compatible agent practices, organizational structures and technological styles may appear but now becomes a burden rather than a boon on economic growth. Agents promote their own narrow bureaucratic interests, the military-industrial organization becomes isolated from the rest of the economy and the technological culture is sheltered from the market and responds primarily to the military challenges emanating from the international strategic environment.

Yet the case studies of Britain and the United States show beyond any doubt that facile conclusion should be avoided; the connection between military industry and economic development is not simple and in no case can a direct causal influence between them be detected. Military R&D and industry, if isolated, are one of the many factors that burden the declining nation's economy. One aspect is the general lack of advanced product innovations, associated with the loss of technological leadership, that would stimulate the economy and enhance its competitiveness in the world market. Military R&D cannot do the job because of its tendency to produce "baroque technologies" in which technical idiosyncrasy, low productivity and high costs are combined (Kaldor 1981, pp. 221-39).

Military forces have a variety of tasks in the external political and commercial relations of the dominant power: they are instruments of rivalry with other major powers and of protection for foreign trade operations. These tasks, in a sense, belong to the very nature of dominant powers, which cannot easily shrug them off even if they try, because that would require the revision of the entire set of national postures and policies. In such a situation, military spending contributes to public overspending that saps and distorts the economic performance in the declining nation. The gradual disappearance of the competitive advantages, combined with high wages and low interest rates, motivates the business community to switch their activities to the export of capital and services. The national economy is converted into a world *rentier* which is pivotal for the smooth operation of the international economy, but which is losing its material power.   Both Britain and the United States have experienced this development during their own careers.

In both of these countries there is evidence that the development of military industry benefited the civilian technology during their industrial rise and heyday. There is an obvious linkage between the economic and political prime of the dominant power and its technological leadership which is, in turn, associated with the control of the leading industrial sectors. This equation of political-military and economic-technological leadership holds only temporarily, however. The ability of the dominant power to maintain its economic and technological leadership is undermined both by its own policies, for example, the exports of capital and technology, and the competitive nature of international environment.

Both the British and US cases suggest that the relative economic decline and the impact of military allocations on it are self-inflicted rather than imposed by the external environment.   True, there is a logic of rising and declining powers and of long economic cycles in the world economy, and it may be difficult to shun its imperatives. Yet one cannot avoid the impression that there has been, both in Britain and the United States, a considerable amount of complacency among the political and economic elites that has influenced the outcome. Perhaps the inability of the political system to provide decisive solutions for the dilemmas plaguing the country is a part of the decline syndrome.

One of the main reasons for the transformation of the positive contribution of military industrialization into a negative one is the isolation of the military R&D and production from the competitive pressures of the market.   The bureaucratic interests of the military, its penchant for custom-made technical solutions and the atmosphere of technological mercantilism all favour the disengagement of military industry from the civilian market. There are considerable differences in the technological styles of military and civilian industry. Also their approaches to innovation differ; the military-industrial approach is accustomed to the limited nature of its risks, ready availability of funds, the lack of competition and the effort to protect the technology from falling into the adversary's hands. The commercial approach is predicated on the need constantly to increase productivity, to adapt the products for the demands of the market and to live with the reality of national and international competition (Derian 1990, pp. 52-8).

Jean-Claude Derian has captured the essential difference between these two technological styles with his concepts of the sheltered culture and the exposed culture. In the military industry the government has created a sheltered environment in which the market structure favours monopolistic competition (Derian 1990, pp. 69-70). The protected nature of the military industry ensures that there is no need, comparable to that of the exposed culture, to increase productivity, to engage in product rather than process innovations and to achieve market share. The isolation and schlerosis of the military industry means, over the long term, that it becomes a drag on the development of the commercial civilian industry and hence on the entire national economy. The military industry undermines the competitive capacity of the economy in the global

106 *Military Industrialization and Economic Development*

marketplace. This effect is more pronounced if the economy is in relative decline and if the growth of the world economy has decelerated.

The only possibility of overcoming the economic dilemmas of a declining country is to radically restructure the economy. The restructuring should, of course, focus primarily on the civilian sector which is usually much bigger than the military-industrial sector. For the military industry this means either the reduction of its size or the reorganization of its technological style and linkages with the civilian sector. Such a restructuring is difficult to implement, because powerful interest groups favour the continuation of the old bureaucratic practices and technological paradigms. In other words, the declining economy has a considerable amount of dead weight.

An empirical study by Karen Rasler and William R. Thompson (1988, pp. 75-81) suggests that the burden of military spending had an insignificant effect on the British hegemonic decline before World War I, while for the United States after World War II there is a significant negative association between these two factors. My case studies do not provide convincing support for this difference between the two system leaders. One could observe, though, that the growth rates of the British leading sectors accelerated in the 1900s in comparison with previous decades, while they decelerated in the United States in the 1970s and the 1980s (Thompson 1990, pp. 228-31). Judged by this criterion the British economy was more dynamic during its system leadership than the US economy.

The difference can be further explained by two factors. The British hegemonic decline occurred, in part, during the upswing of the world economy in the two decades prior to World War I, while the US experiences are explored here during the downswing period of the long cycle. In addition, the United States was involved in a major war in Vietnam which eroded its economy, while Britain did not have a similar experience sapping its energies, expect perhaps for the Boer War at the turn of the century.

Although the relative decline of the British economy is beyond any dispute, it was obviously better able than the United States to insert its military industry into the domestic economic structure. If this is the case, the positive predictions regarding the ability of the United States to preserve its dominant international position in the future may be somewhat too optimistic. While the extent and structure of the military industry is not the most decisive factor in the future US position, much will depend on the administration's ability to scale down and restructure the military establishment in the new international environment.

Bibliography

Abramovitz, Moses, "Catching Up, Forging Ahead, and Falling Behind", *The Journal of Economic History*, 1986, Vol. 46, No. 2, pp. 385-406.

Adams, G. and D. A. Gold, "The Economics of Military Spending: Is the Military Dollar Really Different", in Christian Schmidt and Frank Blackaby (eds), *Peace, Defence and Economic Analysis*, 1987, Macmillan: London, pp. 266-300.

Adler, Emanuel, *The Power of Ideology. The Quest for Technological Autonomy in Argentina and Brazil*, 1987, University of California Press: Berkeley.

Aldcroft, D. H., "Introduction: British Industry and Foreign Competition, 1875-1914", in Derek H. Aldcroft (ed.), *The Development of British Industry and Foreign Competition 1875-1914*, 1968, George Allen and Unwin: London, pp. 11-36.

Allen, G. C., *A Short Economic History of Modern Japan, 1867-1937*, 1962, Unwin University Book: London.

Allen, Robert C., "International Competition in Iron and Steel, 1850-1913", *Journal of Economic History*, 1979, Vol. 39, No. 4, pp. 911-37.

Ando, Yoshio, "The Formation of Heavy Industry", in Seiichi Tobata (ed.), *The Modernization of Japan*, 1966, Vol. 1, Institute of Asian Economic Affairs: Tokyo, pp. 115-35.

Anthony, Ian, Agnès Courades Allenbeck, Esper Gullikstad, Gerd Hagmeyer-Gaverus and Herbert Wulf, "Arms Production", in *SIPRI Yearbook 1990. World Armaments and Disarmament*, 1990, Oxford University Press: Oxford, pp. 317-68.

Armstrong, David A., *Bullets and Bureaucrats. The Machine Gun and the United States Army, 1861-1916*, 1982, Greenwood Press: Westport, Conn.

Arruda, Antonio de, *ESG. Historia de sua doutrina*, Edicoes GRD: São Paulo.

Ayres, Ron, 1983, "Arms Production as a Form of Import-Substituting Industrialization: The Turkish Case", *World Development*, 1983, Vol. 11, No. 9, pp. 813-23.

Ball, Nicole, *Security and Economy in the Third World*, 1988, Princeton University Press: Princeton, NJ.

Banks, Arthur S., *A Cross-Policy Survey*, 1982, MIT Press: Cambridge, MA.

Barnett, Michael, "The High Politics is Low Politics: The Domestic and Systemic Sources of Israeli Security Policy, 1967-1977", *World Politics*, 1990, Vol. 42, No. 4, pp. 529-62.

Barros, Alexandre de S. C., "Brazil", in James Everett Katz (ed.), *Arms Production in Developing Countries*, 1984, Lexington Books: Lexington, Mass., pp. 73-87.

Baumol, Willian J., "Is There a US Productivity Crisis?", *Science*, 1989, Vol. 243, pp. 611-15.

Beasley, W. G., *The Meiji Restoration*, 1972, Stanford University Press: Stanford.

Beasley, W. G., *The Modern History of Japan* (3rd rev. edn), 1982, Charles E. Tuttle Co.: Tokyo.

Beckmann, George M., *The Modernization of China and Japan*, 1962, Harper and Row: New York.

Berghahn, Volker R., *Der Tirpitz-Plan. Genesis und Verfall einer innenpolitische Krisenstrategie unter Wilhelm II*, 1971, Droste: Düsseldorf.

Bertin, Gilles Y. and Sally Wyatt, *Multinationals and Industrial Property. The Control of the World's Technology*, 1988, Harverster: Hemel Hempstead.

Bhagavan, M. R., *Interrelations between Technological Choices and Industrial Strategies in Third World Countries*, 1979, Scandinavian Institute of African Studies, Research Report No. 49, Uppsala.

Blank, Rebecca and Emma Rothschild, "The Effect of the United States Defence Spending on the Employment and Output", *International Labour Review*, 1985, Vol. 124, No. 6, pp. 677-97.

Bradbury, R. H., "The International Impact of Microelectronics", *Science and Public Policy*, 1981, Vol. 8, No. 4, pp. 281-9.

Branco, Lucio Castello, *Staat, Raum und Macht in Brasilien*, 1983, Fink Verlag: München.

Brasseul, Jacques, "Le développement des exportations industrielles du Brézil", *Revue Tiers Monde*, 1981, Vol. 22, No. 1, pp. 141-56.

Brauch, Hans Gunter, "Weapons Innovation and US Strategic Weapons Systems: Learning from Case Studies?", in Nils Petter Gleditsch and Olav Njoelstad (eds), *Arms Races. Technological and Political Dynamics*, 1990, Sage: London, pp. 173-219.

Brigagao, Clóvis, *O mercado da seguranca. Ensaios sobre economia politica da defesa*, 1984, Editora Nova Fronteira: Rio de Janeiro.

Brigagao, Clóvis, *A militarizacao da sociedade*, 1985, Jorge Zahar Editor: Rio de Janeiro.

Brigagao, Clóvis, "The Brazilian Arms Industry", *Journal of International Affairs*, 1986, Vol. 40, No. 1, pp. 101-14.

Brooke, Jim, "Dateline Brazil: Southern Superpower", *Foreign Policy*, 1981, No. 44, pp. 167-80.

Brzoska, Michael, *The Impact of Arms Production in the Third World*, 1987, Centre for the Study of Wars, Armaments and Development, University of Hamburg, Working Paper Series No. 8.

Brzoska, Michael and Peter Lock, "The Effects of Military R&D on North-South Relations: Widening the Gap", *Bulletin of Peace Proposals*, 1988, Vol. 19, Nos. 3-4, pp. 385-97.

Brzoska, Michael and Thomas Ohlson, "Arms Production in the Third World: An Overview", in Brzoska, Michael and Thomas Ohlson (eds), *Arms Production in the Third World*, 1986, Taylor and Francis: London, pp. 7-33.

Burgess, Mike and Daniel Wolf, *The Concept of Power in the Brazilian Higher War College (ESG)*, 1979, LARU Working Paper 27, Latin American Research Unit: University of Toronto.

Buzan, Barry, *An Introduction to Strategic Studies. Military Technology and International Relations*, 1987, St. Martin's Press: New York.

Carey, John, "Will Uncle Sam be Dragged Kicking and Screaming into Lab?", *Business Week*, 1991, July 15, pp. 93-4.

Chan, Steve, "Defense Burden and Economic Growth: Unraveling the Taiwanese Enigma", *American Political Science Review*, 1988, Vol. 82, No. 3, pp. 913-20.

Chesnais, François, Bernard Haudeville, Michelle Fouquin, Christos Passadeos, Yves Perez and Claude Serfati, *Compétitivité internationale et dépense militaires*, 1990, Economica: Paris.

Cheung, Tai Ming, "Disarmament and Development in China. The Relationship between National Defense and Economic Development", *Asian Survey*, 1988, Vol. 28, No. 7, pp. 757-74.

Christensen, Arne Magnus, *Military Research and Development, Technological Change and Civilian Economic Growth*, 1989, PRIO Report, No. 2, Oslo.

Clapham, Sir John, *An Economic History of Modern Britain*, 1951, Cambridge University Press: Cambridge.

Clark, Norman, *The Political Economy of Science and Technology*, 1985, Basil Blackwell: Oxford.

Cochran, Amalia and Michael D. Ward, "Economic Growth and Military Spending in Brazil", 1991. Paper presented to the Annual Convention of the International Studies Association, Vancouver, BC, March.

Cohen Richard and Peter A. Wilson, "Superpowers in Decline? Economic Performance and National Security", *Comparative Strategy*, 1988, Vol. 7, No. 2, pp. 99-132.

Cox, Robert W., *Production, Power and the World Order. Social Forces in the Making of History*, 1987, Columbia University Press: New York.

van Creveld, Martin, *Technology and War. From 2000 B.C to the Present*, 1989, The Free Press: New York.

Crow, Ben and Mary Thorpe, *Survival and Change in the Third World*, 1988, Polity Press: London.

Crowley, James B., "Japan's Military Foreign Policies", in James William Morley (ed.), *Japan's Foreign Policy 1868-1941. A Research Guide*, 1974, Columbia University Press: New York, pp. 3-105.

Cyert, Richard M. and David C. Mowery, "Technology Employment and US Competitiveness", *Scientific American*, 1989, Vol. 260, No. 5, pp. 28-35.

Cypher, James M., "Military Spending, Technical Change and Economic Growth: A Disguised Form of Industrial Policy?", *Journal of Economic Issues*, 1987, Vol. 21, No. 1, pp. 33-59.

Daalder, Ivo H., *The SDI Challenge to Europe*, 1987, Ballinger: Cambridge, Mass.

Davis, Christopher M., "The High-Priority Military Sector in a Shortage Economy", in Henry. S. Rouwen and Charles Wolf, Jr. (eds), *The Impoverished Superpower. Perestroika and the Soviet Military Burden*, 1990, ICS Press: San Francisco, pp. 155-84.

Davis, Lance E. and Robert A. Huttenback, *Mammon and the Pursuit of Empire. The Economics of British Imperialism*, 1988, Cambridge University Press: Cambridge.

Defense Technology Base, *Introduction and Overview. A Special Report of OTA's Assessment on Maintaining the Defense Technology Base*, 1988, Office of Technology Assessment: Washington, DC.

Deger, Saadet and S. Sen, "Defence Industrialization, Technology Transfer and Choice of Techniques in LDCs", in Silvio Borner and Alwyn Taylor (eds.), *Structural Change, Economic Interdependence and World Development*, 1987, Macmillan: London, pp. 233-254.

deGrasse, Robert W., Jr., *Military Expansion, Military Decline*, 1983, Council on Economic Priorities: New York.

Derian, Jean-Claude, *America's Struggle for Leadership in Technology* (trans. by Severen Schaeffer), 1990, The MIT Press: Cambridge, Mass.

Deutsch, Edwin and Wolfgang Schöpp, "Civil versus Military R&D Expenditures and Industrial Productivity", in Christian Schmidt (ed.), *The Economics of Military Expenditures. Military Expenditures, Economic Growth and Fluctuations*, 1987, Macmillan: London, pp. 336-56.

Dickson, David, *The New Politics of Science*, 1988, The University of Chicago Press: Chicago.

diFilippo, Anthony, *Military Spending and Industrial Decline. A Study of the American Machine Tool Industry*, 1986, Greenwood Press: New York.

Dolman, Antony J., *Resources, Regimes, World Order*, 1981, Pergamon Press: New York.

Domke, William K., *War and the Changing Global System*, 1988, Yale University Press: New Haven.

Dosi, Giovanni, "Technological Paradigms and Technological Trajectories", *Research Policy*, 1982, Vol. 11, No. 2.

Dower, John W., "Japan's New Military Edge", *The Nation*, 1989, July 3, pp. 1, 18-22.

van Duijn, Jacob J., *The Long Wave of Economic Life*, 1983, Allen and Unwin: London.

Dumas, Lloyd J., "Military Spending and Economic Decay", in Lloyd J. Dumas (ed.), *The Political Economy of Arms Reduction*, 1982, Westview: Boulder, pp. 1-26.

Dumas, Lloyd J., "Military Research and Development, and Economic Progress: Of Burdens and Opportunities", *Bulletin of Peace Proposals*, 1988, Vol. 19, No. 3-4, pp. 293-303.

Duus, Peter, "Economic Dimensions of Meiji Imperialism: The Case of Korea, 1895-1910", in Ramon H. Myers and Mark R. Peattie (eds), *The Japanese Colonial Empire, 1895-1945*, 1984, Princeton University Press: Princeton, NJ, pp. 128-71.

Egziabher, Tewolde Berhan, *Technology Generation and the Technological Space*, 1982, The United Nations University HSDRRD-4/UNUP-390: Tokyo.

Evans, Carol, "Reappraising Third-World Arms Production", *Survival*, 1986, Vol. 28, No. 2, pp. 99-118.

Evans, Peter, "The Military, the Multinationals and the 'Miracle': The Political Economy of the 'Brazilian Model' of Development", 1974, *Studies in Comparative International Development*, Vol. 9, No. 3, pp. 26-45.

Fallows, James, *National Defense*, 1981, Vintage Books: New York.

Ferguson, Charles H., "Obsolete Arms Production, Obsolescent Military", *The New York Times*, 1986, April 11, p. 19.

Flora, Peter, *State, Economy and Society in Western Europe, 1815-1975*, 1983, Vol. I, Frankfurt am Main: Campus.

Fong, Genn R., "State Strength, Industry Structure and Industrial Policy. American and Japanese Experiences in Microelectronics", *Comparative Politics*, 1990, Vol. 22, No. 3, pp. 273-99.

Frank, Andre Gunder, *Capitalism and Underdevelopment in Latin America*, 1969, Penguin Books: Harmondsworth.

Franko-Jones, Patrice, "'Public-Private Partnership'. Lessons from the Brazilian Armaments Industry", *Journal of Interamerican Studies and Armaments Industry*, 1988, Vol. 29, No. 1, pp. 41-68.

Freeman, Christopher (ed.), *Long Waves in the World Economy*, 1983, Butterworth: London.

French, David, *British Economic and Strategic Planning, 1905-1915*, 1982, Allen and Unwin: London.

Friedberg, Aaron L., *The Weary Titan. Britain and the Experience of Relative Decline, 1895-1905*, 1988, Princeton University Press: Princeton, NJ.

Friedberg, Aaron L., "The Strategic Implications of Relative Economic Decline", *Political Science Quarterly*, 1989, Vol. 104, No. 3, pp. 401-31.

Friedman, Benjamin M., "Reagan Lives!", *The New York Review of Books*, 1990, Vol. 37, No. 20, pp. 29-33.

Fugushima, Shingo, "The Building of National Army", in Seiichi Tobata (ed.), *The Modernization of Japan*, 1966, Vol. 1, The Institute of Asian Economic Affairs: Tokyo, pp. 185-208.

Gamble, Andrew, *Britain in Decline. Economic Policy, Political Strategy and the British State*, 1981, Macmillan: London.

Gamble, Andrew, "Britain"s Decline: Some Theoretical Issues", in Michael Mann (ed.), *The Rise and Decline of the Nation State*, 1990, Basil Blackwell: Oxford, pp. 71-90.

Gansler, Jacques S., *The Defense Industry*, 1980, The MIT Press: Cambridge, Mass.

Gansler, Jacques S., "Needed: A US Defense Industrial Strategy", *International Security*, 1987, Vol. 12, No. 2, pp. 45-62.

Gansler, Jacques S., *Affording Defense*, 1989, The MIT Press: Cambridge, Mass.

Garden, Timothy, *The Technology Trap. Science and the Military*, 1989, Brassey's Defence Publishers: London.

Garon, Sheldon, *The State and Labor in Modern Japan*, 1987, University of California Press: Berkeley.

Gill, Stephen, *American Hegemony and the Trilateral Commission*, 1990, Cambridge University Press: Cambridge.

Gill, Stephen and David Law, "Reflections of Military-Industrial Rivalry in the Global Political Economy", *Millennium*, 1987, Vol. 16, No. 1, pp. 73-86.

Gill, Stephen and David Law, *The Global Political Economy. Perspectives, Problems and Policies*, 1988, The Johns Hopkins University Press: Baltimore.

Gill, Stephen and David Law, "Global Hegemony and the Structural Power of Capital", *International Studies Quarterly*, 1989, Vol. 33, No. 4, pp. 475-99.

Gilpin, Robert, "Has Modern Technology Changed International Politics?", in James N. Rosenau, Vincent Davis and Maurice A. East (eds), *The Analysis of International Politics*, 1972, The Free Press: New York, pp. 166-74.

Gilpin, Robert, *The Political Economy of International Relations*, 1987, Princeton University Press: Princeton, NJ.

Gilpin, Robert, *War and Change in World Politics*, 1981, Cambridge University Press: Cambridge.

Gould, David, *The Impact of Defense Spending on Investment, Productivity and Economic Growth*, 1990, Defense Budget Project: Washington, DC.

Gould, David, "Military R&D. A Poor Scapegoat for Flagging Economy", *The Bulletin of Atomic Scientists*, 1991, Vol. 47, No. 1, pp. 38-43.

Goldfrank, Walter L., "The Limits of Analogy: Hegemonic Decline in Great Britain and the United States", in Albert Bergesen (ed.), *Crises in the World-System*, 1983, Sage: Beverly Hills, pp. 143-54.

Goldstein, Joshua S., *Long Cycles. Prosperity and War in Modern Age*, 1988, Yale University Press: New Haven.

Gourevitch, Peter, *Politics in Hard Times. Comparative Responses to International Economic Crises*, 1986, Cornell University Press: Ithaca, NY.

Gupta, Amit, "The Indian Arms Industry. A Lumbering Giant?", *Asian Survey*, 1990, Vol. 30, No. 9, pp. 846-61.

Hacker, Barton C., "The Weapons of the West. Military Technology and Modernization in 19th-Century China and Japan", *Technology and Culture*, 1977, Vol. 18, No. 1, pp. 43-55.

Haglund, David G. and Marc L. Busch, " 'Techno-Nationalism ' and the Contemporary Debate over the American Defence Industrial Base", in David G. Haglund (ed.), *The Defence Industrial Base and the West*, 1989, Routledge: London, pp. 234-77.

Hall, John A., "Will the United States Decline as did Britain", in Michael Mann, *The Rise and Decline of the Nation State*, 1990, Basil Blackwell: Oxford, pp. 114-45.

Hall, Peter and Paschal Preston, *The Carrier Wave. New Information Technology and the Geography of Innovation 1846-2003*, 1988, Unwin Hyman: London.

Halliday, Jon, *A Political History of Japanese Capitalism*, 1975, Pantheon Books: New York.

Hartley, Keith, "The Evaluation of Efficiency in the Arms Industry", in Silvio Borner and Alwyn Taylor (eds), *Structural Change, Economic Interdependence and World Developement*, 1987, Macmillan: London, pp. 181-201.

Hayashi, Takeshi, *The Japanese Experience in Technology. From Transfer to Self-Reliance*, 1990, The United Nations University Press: Tokyo.

Headrick, Daniel R., *The Tentacles of Progress. Technology Transfer. Technology Transfer in the Age of Imperialism, 1850-1940*, 1988, Oxford University Press: New York.

Henry, David K. and Richard P. Oliver, "The Defense Buildup, 1977-85: Effects on Production and Employment", *Monthly Labor Review*, 1987, Vol. 67, No. 8, pp. 3-11.

Hills, Jill, "Foreign Policy and Technology: The Japan-US, Japan-Britain and Japan-EEC Technology Agreements", *Political Studies*, 1983, Vol. 31, No. 3, pp. 205-23.

Hilton, Stanley, "Military Influence on Brazilian Economic Policy, 1930-1945: A Different View", *Hispanic American Historical Review*, 1973, Vol. 53, No. 1, pp. 71-94.

Hilton, Stanley, "The Armed Forces and Industrialists in Modern Brazil: The Drive for Military Autonomy (1889-1954)", *Hispanic American Historical Review*, 1982, Vol. 62, No. 4, pp. 629-73.

Hirschmeier, Johannes and Tsunehiko Yui, *The Development of Japanese Business 1600-1973*, 1975, George Allen and Unwin: London.

Hoag, Paul W., "Hi-Tech Armaments, Space Militarization and the Third World", in Colin Creighton and Martin Shaw (eds), *The Sociology of War and Peace*, 1987, Macmillan: London, pp. 73-96.

Hobsbawn, Eric, *Industry and Empire. From 1750 to the Present Day*, 1968, Pelican: Harmondsworth.

Holland, Max, *When the Machine Stopped. A Cautionary Tale from Industrial America*, 1989, Harvard Business School Press: Cambridge, Mass.

Hoyt, Edwin P., *The Militarists. The Rise of Japanese Militarism since WW II*, 1985, Donald I. Fine: New York.

Hsu, Immanuel, *The Rise of Modern China* (3rd edn), 1983, Oxford University Press: Oxford.

Hunter, Janet E., *The Emergence of Modern Japan*, 1989, Longman: London.

Ikeda, Kiyoshi, "The Douglas Mission and British Influence on the Japanese Navy", in Sue Henry and Jean-Pierre Lehmann (eds), *Themes and Theories in Modern Japanese History*, 1988, The Athlone Press: London, pp. 172-84.

Inman, B. R. and Daniel F. Burton, Jr., "Technology and Competitiveness: The New Policy Frontier", *Foreign Affairs*, 1990, Vol. 69, No. 2, pp. 116-34.

Jansen, Marius B., *Sakamoto Ryoma and the Meiji Restoration*, 1971, Stanford University Press: Stanford.

Jansen, Marius B., "Japanese Imperialism. Late Meiji Perspectives", in Ramon H. Myers and Mark R. Peattie (eds), *The Japanese Colonial Empire, 1895-1940*, 1984, Princeton, NJ, pp. 61-79.

Johnson, Chalmers, *MITI and the Japanese Miracle*, Stanford University Press: Stanford.

Johnson, Franklyn Arthur, *Defence by Committee. The British Committee of Imperial Defence 1885-1959*, 1960, Oxford University Press: London.

Jones, R. J. Barry, "Economic Realism, Neo-Ricardin Structuralism and the Political Economy of Contemporary Neo-Mercantilism", in R. J. Barry Jones (ed.), *The Worlds of Political Economy*, 1988, Pinter: London, pp. 142-68.

Junne, Gerd, "Die amerikanische Rüstungspolitik. Ein Substitut für Industriepolitik", *Leviathan*, 1985, Vol. 13, No. 1, pp. 23-37.

Kahler, Miles, "External Ambition and Economic Performance", *World Politics*, 1988, Vol. 40, No. 4, pp. 419-51.

Kaldor, Mary, *The Baroque Arsenal*, 1981, Hill and Wang: New York.

Kaldor, Mary, "The Atlantic Technology Culture", in Mary Kaldor and Richard Falk (eds), *Dealignment. A New Foreign Policy Perspective*, 1987, Basil Blackwell, Oxford, pp. 143-62.

Kapstein, Ethan B., "The Brazilian Defense Industry and the International System", *Political Science Quarterly*, 1991, Vol. 105, No. 4, pp. 578-96.

Kennedy Paul M., *Realities Behind Diplomacy. Background Influences on British External Policy 1865-1980*, 1981, Glasgow: Fontana.

Kennedy Paul M., *The Rise of the Anglo-German Antagonism 1860-1914*, 1982, George Allen and Unwin: London.

Kennedy Paul M., *The Rise and Fall of Great Powers. Economic Change and Military Conflict from 1500 to 2000*, 1987, Random House: New York.

Kirby, M. W., *The Decline of the British Economic Power since 1870*, 1981, George Allen and Unwin: London.

Köhler, Gernot, "Determinants of the British Defense Burden 1689-1977", *Bulletin of Peace Proposals*, 1980, Vol. 11, No. 1, pp. 79-85.

Kolodziej, Edward A., "Re-evaluating Economic and Technological Variables to Explain Global Arms Production and Sales", in Christian Schmidt (ed.), *The Economics of Military Expenditures. Military Expenditures, Economic Growth and Fluctuations*, 1987, Macmillan: London, pp. 304-35.

Kubbig, Bernd W., "Military-Civilian Spin-Off: "Promises, Premises and Problems", *Development and Peace*, 1986, Vol. 7, No. 2, pp. 199-227.

Kubbig, Bernd W., *Die SDI-Rahmenvereinbarung zwischen Bonn und Washington. Eine Bilanz nach zwei Jahren*, 1988, Hessische Stiftung Friedens-und Konfliktforschung. Report 3: Frankfurt am Main.

Kurth, James R., "The Political Consequences of the Product Cycle: Industrial History and Political Outcomes", *International Organization*, 1979, Vol. 33, No. 1, pp. 1-34.

Kuttner, Robert, *The End of Laissez Faire. National Purpose and the Global Economy after the Cold War*, 1991, Alfred A. Knopt: New York.

Lake, David A., *Power, Protection and Free Trade. International Sources of US Commercial Strategy. 1887-1939*, 1988, Cornell University Press: Ithaca, NY.

Landes, David, *The Unbound Prometheus. Technological Change and Industrial Development in Western Europe from 1750 to the Present*, 1981, Cambridge University Press: Cambridge (first published in 1969).

Lehmann, Jean-Pierre, *The Roots of Modern Japan*, 1982, Macmillan: London.

Lindgren, Göran, *Armaments and Economic Performance in Industrialized Market Economies*, 1985, Department of Peace and Conflict Research, Uppsala University, Report No. 26.

Lindgren, Göran, "Armaments and Economic Performance", in Peter Wallensteen (ed.), *Peace Research. Achievements and Challenges*, Westview Press: Boulder, pp. 169-215.

Lock, Peter, "Brazil: Arms for Exports", in Michael Brzoska and Thomas Ohlson (eds), *Arms Production in the Third World*, 1986, Taylor and Francis: London, pp. 79-104.

Lockwood, William W., *The Economic Development of Japan. Growth and Structural Change 1868-1954*, 1954, Princeton University Press: Princeton, NJ.

Lucas, Michael R., *The Western Alliance after INF. Redefining US Policy toward Europe and the Soviet Union*, 1990, Lynne Rienner: Boulder.

McCann, Frank D., Jr., "The Brazilian Army and the Problem of Mission, 1939-1964", *Journal of Latin American Studies*, 1980, Vol. 12, No. 1, pp. 107-26.

McCann, Frank D., "The Formative Period of Twentieth Century Brazilian Army Thought, 1900-1922", *Hispanic American Historical Review*, 1984, Vol. 64, No. 4, pp. 737-65.

McMichael, Philip, "Britain's Hegemony in the Nineteenth-Century and World-Economy", in Peter Evans, Dietrich Rueschmayer (eds), *States versus Markets in the World-System*, 1985, Sage: Beverly Hills, pp. 117-50.

McNeill, William, *The Pursuit of Power. Technology, Armed Forces, and Society since A.D. 1000*, 1982, The University of Chicago Press: Chicago.

Maddison, Angus, *Phases of Capitalist Development*, 1982, Oxford University Press: Oxford.

Mandelbaum, Michael, *The Fate of Nations. The Search for National Security in the Nineteenth and Twentieth Centuries*, 1988, Cambridge University Press: Cambridge.

Mansfield, Edwin, "Technology and Productivity in the United States", in Martin Feldstein (ed.), *The American Economy in Transition*, 1980, The University of Chicago Press: Chicago, pp. 563-96.

Markusen, Anne, "The Militarized Economy", *World Policy Journal*, 1986, Vol. 3, No. 3, pp. 495-516.

Marshall, Byron K., *Capitalism and Nationalism in Prewar Japan. The Ideology of Business Elite, 1868-1941*, 1967, Stanford University Press: Stanford.

Mastanduno, Michael, David A. Lake and G. John Ikenberry, "Toward a Realist Theory of State Action", *International Studies Quarterly*, 1989, Vol. 33, No. 4, pp. 457-74.

Mathias, Peter, *The First Industrial Nation. An Economic History of Britain 1700-1914*, 1983, Methuen: London.

Matthews, R. C. O., C. H. Feinstein and J. C. Odling-Smee, *British Economic Growth 1856-1973*, 1982, Clarendon Press: Oxford.

Melman, Seymour, *The Permanent War Economy*, 1974, Simon and Schuster: New York.

Mettler, Ruben F., "Technology: A Powerful Agent for Change", in Martin Feldstein (ed.), *The American Economy in Transition*, 1980, The University of Chicago Press: Chicago, pp. 596-604.

Mintz, Alex, "Military-Industrial Linkages in Israel", *Armed Forces and Society*, 1985, Vol. 12, No. 1, pp. 9-27.

Misa, Thomas J., "Military Needs, Commercial Realities, and the Development of the Transistor, 1948-1958", in Merritt Roe Smith (ed.), *Military Enterprise and Technological Change. Perspectives on the American Experience*, 1985, The MIT Press: Cambridge, MA, pp. 253-87.

Mitsukuni, Yoshida, "The Restoration and the History of Technology", in Nagai Michio and Miguel Urrutia (eds), *Meiji Ishin: Restoration and Revolution*, 1985, The United Nations University: Tokyo, pp. 192-204.

Miyake, Masaki, "German Cultural and Political Influence on Japan, 1870-1914", in John A. Moses and Paul M. Kennedy (eds), *Germany in the Pacific and Far East, 1870-1914*, 1977, University of Queensland Press: St. Lucia, pp. 156-81.

Modelski, George and William Thompson R., *Seapower in Global Politics 1494-1993*, 1987, Macmillan: Basingstoke.

Mokyr, Joel, *The Lever of Riches. Technological Creativity and Economic Progress*, 1990, Oxford University Press: Oxford.

Moltmann, Bernhard, "Brazilian: Zwanzig Jahre Militärherrschaft - Lange Schatten eines ehrgeizigen Entwicklungsmodells", in Reiner Steinweg (ed.), *Militärregime und Entwicklungspolitik*, 1989, Suhrkamp: Frankfurt am Main, pp. 85-103.

Moran, Theodore H., "The Globalization of America's Defense Industries: Managing the Threat of Foreign Dependence", *International Security*, 1990, Vol. 15, No. 1, pp. 57-99.

Mullins, A. F. Jr., *Born Arming. Development and Military Power in New States*, 1987, Stanford University Press: Stanford.

Nau, Henry R., *The Myth of America's Decline. Leading the World Economy into the 1990's*, 1990, Oxford University Press: New York.

Nef, John U., *War and Human Progress. An Essay on the Rise of Industrial Civilization*, 1978, W.W. Northon: New York (first published in 1950).

Nelson, Richard R. and Sidney, G. Winter, "In Search for a Useful Theory of Innovation", *Research Policy*, 1977, Vol. 6, No. 1.

Neumann, Stephanie, "International Stratification and the Third World Military Industries", *International Organizations*, 1984, Vol. 38, No. 2, pp. 167-97.

Newton, Wesley Phillips, "International Aviation Rivalry in Latin America, 1919-1927", *Journal of Inter-American Studies*, 1965, Vol. 7, No. 3, pp. 345-56.

Nishikawa, Shunsaku and Osamu Saito, "The Economic History of the Restoration Period", in Michio Nagai and Miguel Urrutia (eds), *Meiji Ishin: Restoration and Revolution*, 1985, The United Nations University: Tokyo, pp. 175-91.

Noble, David F., "Command Performance: A Perspective on the Social and Economic Consequences of Military Enterprise", in Merrit Roe Smith (ed.), *Military Enterprise and Technological Change. Perspectives on the American Experience*, 1987, The MIT Press: Cambridge, MA, pp. 328-46.

Nolan, Janne E., *Military Industry, in Taiwan and South Korea*, 1986, Macmillan: London.

Norman, E. Herbert, *Japan's Emergence as a Modern State. Political and Economic Problems of the Meiji Period*, 1940, Institute of Pacific Relations: New York.

Nye, Joseph S., Jr., *Bound to Lead. The Changing Nature of American Power*, 1990, Basic Books: New York.

Nzongola-Ntalaja and Laura Bigman, "The Arms Race and the Process of National Reconstruction in Developing Countries", *UNESCO Yearbook on Peace and Conflict Studies 1987*, 1989, Greenwood Press: Westport, Conn., pp. 219-71.

O'Brien, Patrick K., "The Imperial Component of the British Economy before 1914", in Michael Mann (ed.), *The Rise and Decline of the Nation State*, 1990, Basil Blackwell: Oxford, pp. 12-46.

Ohmae, Kenichi, *The Borderless World. Power and Strategy in the Interlinked Economy*, 1990, Harper Business: New York.

Paris, Michael, "Air Power and Imperial Defence 1880-1919", *Journal of Contemporary History*, 1989, Vol. 24. No. 2, pp. 209-25.

Payne, P. L., "Iron and Steel Manufactures", in Derek H. Aldcroft (ed.), *The Development of British Industry and Foreign Competition 1875-1914*, 1968, George Allen and Unwin: London, pp. 71-99.

Pearton, Maurice, *The Knowledgeable State. Diplomacy, War and Technology since 1830*, 1982, Burnett Books: London.

Peleg, Ivan, "Military Production in Third World Countries: A Political Study", in Pat McGowan and Charles W. Kegley, Jr. (eds), *Threats, Weapons and Foreign Policy*, 1980, Sage: Beverly Hills, pp. 209-30.

Perry, William, J., "The Brazilian Armed Forces: Military Policy and Conventional Capabilities of an Emerging Power", *Military Review*, 1978, Vol. 58, No. 9, pp. 10-24.

Perry, William, J., "Defense Investment Strategy", *Foreign Affairs*, 1989, Vol. 68, No. 2, pp. 72-92.

Pianta, Mario, *New Techonologies Across the Atlantic. US Leadership or European Autonomy?*, 1988, Harvester: Hemel Hempstead.

Pollard, Sidney, *Britain's Prime and Britain's Decline. The British Economy 1870-1914*, 1989, Edward Arnold: London.

Porter, Bernard, *Britain, Europe and the World 1850-1982: Delusions of Grandeur*, 1983, Allen and Unwin: London.

Porter, Michael E., *The Competitive Advantage of Nations*, 1990, The Free Press: New York.

Prestowitz, Clyde V., Jr., *Trading Places. How America Allowed Japan to Take the Lead*, 1988, Charles E. Tuttle: Tokyo.

Ramo, Simon, "Globalization of Industry and Implications for the Future", in Janet H. Muroyama and H. Guyford Stever (eds), *Globalization of Technology. International Perspectives*, 1988, National Academy Press: Washington, DC, pp. 12-22.

Ramses 90, *Rapport annuel mondial sur le système économique et les stratégies*, 1989, Institut français des relations internationales: Paris.

Rasler, Karen and William R. Thompson, "Defense Burdens, Capital Formation, and Economic Growth", *Journal of Conflict Resolution*, 1988, Vol. 32., No. 1, pp. 61-86.

Reppy, Judith, "Military R&D and Civilian Economy", *Bulletin of Atomic Scientists*, 1985, Vol. 41, No. 10, pp. 10-14.

Revuelta, Klaus Wolff-Casado, "The Brazilian Defence Industry", *Military Technology*, 1985, Vol. 9, No. 10, pp. 92-119.

Reynolds, Charles, *The Politics of War. A Study of the Rationality of Violence in Inter-State Relations*, 1989, Harvester: Hemel Hempstead.

Rice, Richard, "Comment", *Journal of Economic History*, 1977, Vol. 37, No. 1, pp. 136-38.

Robbin, Keith, *The Eclipse of a Great Power. Modern Britain 1870-1975*, 1983, Longman: London.

Rosecrance, Richard, *America's Economic Resurgence. A Bold New Strategy*, 1990, Harper and Row: New York.

Rosen, Stephen Peter, "New Ways of War: Understanding Military Innovation", *International Security*, 1988, Vol. 13, No. 1, pp. 134-68.

Rosenberg, Nathan and Claudio R. Frischtak, "Technological Innovation and Long Waves", *Cambridge Journal of Economics*, 1984, Vol. 8, No. 1, pp. 7-24.

Rostow, W. W., "Kontradieff, Schumpeter and Kuznets: Trend Periods Revisited", *Journal of Economic History*, 1975, Vol. 25, No. 4, pp. 719-53.

Rostow, W. W., *The World Economy. History and Prospects*, 1978, University of Texas Press: Austin.

Rozman, Gilbert, "The Rise of the State in China and Japan", in Michael Mann (ed.), *The Rise and Decline of the Nation State*, 1990, Basil Blackwell: Oxford, pp. 172-87.

Russett, Bruce M., "Defense Expenditures and National Well-being", *American Political Science Review*, 1982, Vol. 76, No. 4, pp. 767-76.

Russett, Bruce M., "The Mysterious Case of Vanishing Hegemony; or is Mark Twain Really Dead?", *International Organization*, 1985, Vol. 39, No. 2, pp. 207-231.

Sandberg, L. G., "The Entrepreneur and Technological Change", in Roderick Floud and Donald McCloskey (eds), *The Economic History of Britain Since 1700*, 1981, Cambridge University Press: Cambridge, pp. 99-120.

Saul, S. B. "The Engineering Industry", in Derek H. Aldcroft (ed.), *The Development of British Industry and Foreign Competition 1875-1914*, 1968, Allen and Unwin: London, pp. 186-237.

Schomacker, Klaus, Peter Wilke and Herbert Wulf, *Alternative Produktion statt Rüstung*, 1987, Bund-Verlag: Köln.

Seabury, Paul, "Industrial Policy and National Defense", *Journal of Contemporary Studies*, Vol. 6, No. 1, pp. 5-15.

Searle, G. R., *The Quest for National Efficiency. A Study of British Politics and British Political Thought 1899-1914*, 1971, Basil Blackwell: Oxford.

Sen, Gautam, *The Military Origins of Industrialization and International Trade Rivalry*, 1984, Frances Pinter: London.

Shaw, Bradley T., "Technology and Military Criteria: Broadening the Theory of Innovation", *Technological Forecasting and Social Change*, 1987, Vol. 31, No. 2, pp. 239-56.

Shinohara, Miyohei, "Japan as a World Economic Power", *The Annals of the American Academy of Political and Economic Science*, 1991, Vol. 513, pp. 12-24.

Shunsaku, Nishikawa and Osamu Saito, "The Economic History of the Restoration Period", in Nagai, Michio and Miguel Urrutia (eds.), *Meiji Ishin: Restoration and Revolution*, 1985, The United Nations University: Tokyo, pp. 175-191.

Simkins, Peter, "Kitchener and the Expansion of the Army", in Ian F. W. Beckett and John Gooch (eds), *Politicians and Defence: Studies in the Formulation of British Defence Policy*, 1981, Manchester University Press: Manchester, pp. 87-109.

Skidmore, Thomas E., *Politics in Brazil, 1930-1964: An Experiment in Democracy*, 1967, Oxford University Press: New York.

Skidmore, Thomas E., *The Politics of Military Rule in Brazil, 1964-1985*, 1988, Oxford University Press: Oxford.

Smith, Merritt Roe, "Army Ordnance and the 'American System' of Manufacturing, 1815-1861", in Merritt Roe Smith (ed.), *Military Enterprise and Technological Change. Perspective on the American Experience*, 1987, The MIT Press: Cambridge, Mass., pp. 39-86.

Solomou, Solomos, *Phases of Economic Growth 1850-1973. Kontradieff Waves and Kuznets Swings*, 1988, Cambridge University Press: Cambridge.

Sombart, Werner, *Der moderne Kapitalismus*, Erster Band, 1913, Verlag von Duncker & Humblot: Leipzig.

Spiers, Edward M., *The Army and Society 1815-1914*, 1980, Longman: London.

Stein, Jay M., "Militarism and a Domestic Planning Issue", *International Journal of Urban and Regional Research*, 1985, Vol. 9, No. 3, pp. 341-51.

Stepan, Alfred, *Rethinking Military Politics: Brazil and the Southern Cone*, 1988, Princeton University Press, Princeton, NJ.

Stowsky, Jay, "Competing with Pentagon", *World Policy Journal*, 1986, Vol. 3, No. 4, pp. 697-721.

Strange, Susan, "The Persistent Myth of Lost Hegemony", *International Organization*, 1987, Vol. 41, No. 4, pp. 553-74.

Thee, Marek, *Military Technology, Military Strategy and the Arms Race*, 1986, Croom Helm: London.

Thee, Marek, *Science and Technology: Between Civilian and Military Research and Development*, 1990, UNIDIR Research Paper No. 7, The United Nations: New York.

Thomas, Raju G. C., "US Transfers of 'Dual-Use' Technologies to India", *Asian Survey*, 1990, Vol. 30, No. 9, pp. 825-45.

Thompson, William R., "Long Waves, Innovation, and Decline", *International Organization*, 1990, Vol. 44, No. 2, pp 201-33.

Topik, Steven, "The Evolution of the Economic Role of the Brazilian State, 1889-1930", *Journal of Latin American Studies*, 1979, Vol. 11, No. 2, pp. 323-42.

Trebilcock, Clive, "'Spin-Off' in British Economic History: Armaments and Industry, 1760-1914", *The Economic History Review*, 1969, Vol. 22, No. 2, pp. 474-90.

Trebilcock, Clive, "War and the Failure of Industrial Mobilization: 1899 and 1914", in J. M. Winter (ed.), *War and Economic Development*, 1975, Cambridge University Press: Cambridge, pp. 139-64.

Trebilcock, Clive, "The British Armament Industry 1890-1914: False Legend and True Utility", in Geoffrey Best and Andrew Wheatcroff (eds), *War, Economy and the Military Mind*, 1976, Croom Helm: London, pp. 89-107.

van Tulder, Rob and Gerd Junne, *European Multinationals and Core Technologies*, 1988, John Wiley: New York.

Tuomi, Helena and Raimo Väyrynen, *Transnational Corporations, Armaments and Development*, 1982, Gower: Aldershot.

United Nations, *Study on the Economic and Social Consequences of the Arms Race and Military Expenditures*, 1988, General Assembly A/43/368, The United Nations: New York.

Varga, E. S., "Rüstungswirtschaft und Technik", in E. S. Varga, *Ausgewählte Schriften 1918-1964. Zweiter Band: Die Wirtschaftskrisen*, 1982, Pahl-Rugenstein Verlag: Köln, pp. 453-62.

Väyrynen, Raimo, *Las corporaciones transnacionales y las transferencias de armas*, 1978, Cuadernos semetrales (Mexico).

Väyrynen, Raimo, "Economic Fluctuations, Technological Innovations and Arms Races in Historical Perspectives", *Cooperation and Conflict*, 1983, Vol. 18, No. 3, pp. 135-59.

Väyrynen, Raimo, "World Economy and Geopolitics: The Case of Brazil", in Volker Bornschier and Peter Lengyel (eds), *World Society Studies*, 1989, Vol. I, Campus Verlag: Frankfurt/New York, pp. 131-80.

Väyrynen, Raimo, "Economy, Power and the Arms Race", in Nils Petter Gleditsch and Olave Njoelstad (eds), *Arms Races. Technological and Political Dynamics*, 1990, Sage: London, pp. 314-38.

Veblen, Thorstein, *An Inquiry into the Nature of Peace and the Terms of its Perpetuation*, 1917, Macmillan: London.

Veblen, Thorstein, *Imperial Germany and the Industrial Revolution*, 1915, B.W. Huesch: New York.

Wainstein, Leonard, "The Dreadnought Gap", in Robert J. Art and Kenneth N. Waltz (eds), *The Use of Force. International Politics and Foreign Policy*, 1971, Little, Brown and Co.: Boston, pp. 153-69.

Walsh, Vivien, "Technology and Competitiveness of Small Countries: A Review", in Christopher Freeman and Bengt-Ake Lundwall (eds), *Small Countries Facing the Technological Revolution*, 1988, Pinter: London, pp. 37-66.

Watarai, Toshikaru, *Nationalization of Railways in Japan*, 1915, Columbia University Press: New York.

Weida, William J. and Frank L. Gertcher, *The Political Economy of National Defense*, 1986, Westview Press: Boulder.

Westney, D. Eleanor, *Imitation and Innovation. The Transfer of Western Organizational Patterns of Meiji Japan*, 1987, Harvard University Press: Cambridge, Mass.

Wiener, Martin, J., *English Culture and the Decline of the Industrial Spirit 1850-1980*, 1981, Penguin: Harmondsworth.

Winner Langdon, *The Whale and the Reactor. A Search for Limits in the Age of High Technology*, 1986, Chicago University Press: Chicago.

Wirth, John D., *The Politics of Brazilian Development, 1930-1954*, 1970, Stanford University Press: Stanford.

Wöhlcke, Mandred, *Brazilien als Produzent und Exporteur von Rüstungsgütern*, 1987, Nomos: Baden-Baden.

Wolff, Edward N., "The Magnitude and Causes of the Recent Productivity Slowdown in the United States: A Survey of Recent Studies", in William J. Baumol and Kenneth McLennan (eds), *Productivity Growth and US Competitiveness*, 1985, Oxford University Press: New York, pp. 29-57.

World Armaments and Disarmament. SIPRI Yearbook, 1987, Oxford University Press: Oxford.

World Armaments and Disarmament. SIPRI Yearbook, 1989, Oxford University Press: Oxford.

Wulf, Herbert, "Arms Industry Unlimited: The Economic Impact of the Arms Sector in Developing Countries", *Peace and Development*, 1984, Vol. 5, No. 1, pp. 114-26.

Yamamura, Kozo, "Success Illgotten? The Role of Meiji Militarism in Japan's Technological Progress", *Journal of Economic History*, 1977, Vol. 37, No. 1, pp. 113-35.

UNIDIR Publications
(from 1987)

Research Reports

La guerre des satellites : enjeux pour la communauté internationale, par Pierre Lellouche, éd. (IFRI), Genève, UNIDIR, 1987, 42 p., publication des Nations Unies, numéro de vente: GV.F.87.0.1. Also available in English: *Satellite Warfare: A Challenge for the International Community*.

The International Non-Proliferation Régime 1987, by David A.V. Fischer, Geneva, UNIDIR, 1987, 81 p., United Nations publication, Sales No. GV.E.87.0.2.

La question de la vérification dans les négociations sur le désarmement aux Nations Unies, par Ellis Morris, Genève, UNIDIR, 1987, 230 p., publication des Nations Unies, numéro de vente: GV.F.87.0.4. Also available in English: *The Verification Issue in United Nations Disarmament Negotiations*.

Confidence-Building Measures in Africa, by Augustine P. Mahiga and Fidelis Nji, Geneva, UNIDIR, 1987, 16 p., United Nations publication, Sales No. GV.E.87.0.5

Disarmament: Problems Related to Outer Space, Geneva, UNIDIR, 1987, 190 p., United Nations publication, Sales No. GV.E.87.0.7. Existe aussi en français: *Désarmement: problèmes relatifs à l'espace extra-atmosphérique*.

Interrelationship of Bilateral and Multilateral Disarmament Negotiations / Les relations entre les négociations bilatérales et multilatérales sur le désarmement, Proceedings of the Baku Conference, 2-4 June 1987 / Actes de la conférence de Bakou, 2-4 juin 1987, Geneva, UNIDIR, 1988, 258 p., United Nations publication, Sales No. GV.E./F.88.0.1.

Disarmament Research: Agenda for the 1990's / La recherche sur le désarmement: Programme pour les années 90, Proceedings of the Sochi Conference, 22-24 March 1988 / Actes de la conférence de Sotchi, 22-24 mars 1988, Geneva, UNIDIR, 1988, 165 p., United Nations publication, Sales No. GV.E./F.88.0.3.

Conventional Disarmament in Europe, by André Brie (IIB), Andrzej Karkoszka (PISM), Manfred Müller (IIB), Helga Schirmeister (IIB), Geneva, UNIDIR, 1988, 66 p., United Nations publication, Sales No. GV.E.88.0.6. Existe également en français : *Le désarmement classique en Europe*, 1989, 90 p., publication des Nations Unies, numéro de vente: GV.E.89.0.6.

Arms Transfers and Dependence, by Christian Catrina, published for UNIDIR by Taylor & Francis (New York, London), 1988, 409 p.

Les forces classiques en Europe et la maîtrise des armements, par Pierre Lellouche et Jérôme Paolini, eds. (IFRI), 1989, 88 p, publication des Nations Unies, numéro de vente: GV.F.89.0.6. Also available in English: *Conventional Forces and Arms Limitation in Europe*.

National Security Concepts of States: New Zealand, by Kennedy Graham, published for UNIDIR by Taylor & Francis (New York, London), 1989, 180 p.

Problems and Perspectives of Conventional Disarmament in Europe, Proceedings of the Geneva Conference 23-25 January 1989, published for UNIDIR by Taylor & Francis (New York, London), 1989, 140 p. Existe aussi en français: *Désarmement classique en Europe, Problèmes et perspectives*, publié pour l'UNIDIR et l'IFRI par Masson (Paris), 1990, 226 p.

The Projected Chemical Weapons Convention: A Guide to the Negotiations in the Conference on Disarmament, by Thomas Bernauer, 1990, 328 p., United Nations publication, Sales No. GV.E.90.0.3.

Verification: The Soviet Stance, its Past, Present and Future, by Mikhail Kokeev and Andrei Androsov, 1990, 131 p., United Nations publication, Sales No. GV.E.90.0.6. Existe également en français: *Vérification: la position soviétique - Passé, présent et avenir*, 1990, 145 p., numéro de vente: GV.F.90.0.6.

UNIDIR Repertory of Disarmament Research: 1990, by Chantal de Jonge Oudraat and Péricles Gasparini Alves (eds.), 1990, 402 p., United Nations publication, Sales No. GV.E.90.0.10.

Nonoffensive Defense: A Global Perspective, published for UNIDIR by Taylor & Francis (New York, London), 1990, 194 p.

Aerial Reconnaissance for Verification of Arms Limitation Agreements - An Introduction, by Allan V. Banner, Keith W. Hall and Andrew J. Young, D.C.L., 1990, 166 p., United Nations publication, Sales No. GV.E.90.0.11.

Africa, Disarmament and Security / Afrique, désarmement et sécurité, Proceedings of the Conference of African Research Institutes, 24-25 March 1990 / Actes de la Conférence des Instituts de recherche africains, 24-25 mars 1990, UNIDIR, United Nations publication, Sales No. GV.E/F.91.0.1.

Peaceful and Non-Peaceful Uses of Space: Problems of Definition for the Prevention of an Arms Race, by Bhupendra Jasani (ed.), 1991, 179 p., published for UNIDIR by Taylor & Francis (New York, London).

In Pursuit of a Nuclear Test Ban Treaty: A Guide to the Debate in the Conference on Disarmament, by Thomas Schmalberger, 1991, 132 p., United Nations publication, Sales No. GV.E.91.0.4.

Confidence-building Measures and International Security: The Political and Military Aspect - A Soviet Approach, by Igor Scherbak, 1991, 179 p., United Nations publication, Sales No. GV.E.91.0.7.

Verification of Current Disarmament and Arms Limitation Agreements: Ways, Means and Practices, by Serge Sur (ed.), published for UNIDIR by Dartmouth (Aldershot), 1991, 396 p. Existe également en français: *La vérification des accords sur le désarmement et la limitation des armements : moyens, méthodes et pratiques*, 1991, 406 p., publication des Nations Unies, numéro de vente: GV.F.91.0.9.

The United Nations, Disarmament and Security: Evolution and Prospects, by Jayantha Dhanapala (ed.), 1991, 156 p., United Nations publication, Sales No. GV.E.91.0.13.

Disarmament Agreements and Negotiations: The Economic Dimension, by Serge Sur (ed.), published for UNIDIR by Dartmouth (Aldershot), 1991, 228 p. Existe également en français: *Dimensions économiques des négociations et accords sur le désarmement*, 1991, 211 p., par Serge Sur (éd.), publication des Nations Unies, numéro de vente: GV.F.91.0.18.

Prevention of an Arms Race in Outer Space: A Guide to the Discussions in the Conference on Disarmament, by Péricles Gasparini Alves, 1991, 221 p., United Nations publication, Sales No. GV.E.91.0.17.

Nuclear Issues on the Agenda of the Conference on Disarmament, by Thomas Bernauer, 1991, 108 p., United Nations publication, Sales No. GV.E.91.0.16.

Economic Adjustment after the Cold War: Strategies for Conversion, by Michael Renner, published for UNIDIR by Dartmouth (Aldershot), 1991, 262 p. (**forthcoming**)

Verification of Disarmament or Limitation of Armaments: Instruments, Negotiations, Proposals, by Serge Sur (ed.), United Nations publication (**forthcoming**)

National Security Concepts of Argentina, by Julio C. Carasales, United Nations publication (**forthcoming**)

National Security Concepts of Sri Lanka, by Vernon L. B. Mendis, United Nations publication (**forthcoming**)

Nonmilitary Aspects of Security: A System Approach, by Dietrich Fischer, United Nations publication (**forthcoming**)

European Security in the 1990s: Problems of Southeast Europe, Proceedings of the Rhodes Conference, 6 and 7 September 1991 / Actes de la conférence de Rhodes, 6 et 7 septembre 1991, publication des Nations Unies (**forthcoming**)

Towards 1995: The Prospects for Ending the Proliferation of Nuclear Weapons, by David Fischer (**forthcoming**)

Research Papers

No. 1 -   *Une approche juridique de la vérification en matière de désarmement ou de limitation des armements*, par Serge Sur, septembre 1988, 70 p., publication des Nations Unies, numéro de vente: GV.F.88.0.5. Also available in English: *A Legal Approach to Verification in Disarmament or Arms Limitation*,

No. 2 -   *Problèmes de vérification du Traité de Washington du 8 décembre 1987 sur l'élimination des missiles à portée intermédiaire*, par Serge Sur, octobre 1988, 64 p., publication des Nations Unies, numéro de vente: GV.F.88.0.7. Also available in English: *Verification Problems of the Washington Treaty on the Elimination of Intermediate-Range Missiles.*

No. 3 -   *Mesures de confiance de la CSCE: Documents et commentaires*, par Victor-Yves Ghébali, mars 1989, 112 p., publication des Nations Unies, numéro de vente: GV.F.89.0.5. Also available in English: *Confidence-Building Measures within the CSCE Process: Paragraph-by-Paragraph Analysis of the Helsinki and Stockholm Régimes*, 1989, 110 p., United Nations publication, Sales No. GV.E.89.0.5.

No. 4 -   *The Prevention of the Geographical Proliferation of Nuclear Weapons: Nuclear-Free Zones and Zones of Peace in the Southern Hemisphere*, by Edmundo Fujita, April 1989, 52 p., United Nations publication, Sales No. GV.E. 89.0.8. Existe également en français: *La prévention de la prolifération géographique des armes nucléaires: zones exemptes d'armes nucléaires et zones de paix dans l'hémisphère Sud*, 1989, 61 p., publication des Nations Unies, numéro de vente: GV.F.89.0.8.

No. 5 -   *The Future Chemical Weapons Convention and its Organization: The Executive Council*, by Thomas Bernauer, May 1989, 34 p., United Nations publication, Sales No. GV.E.89.0.7. Existe également en français: *La future convention sur les armes chimiques et son organisation: le Conseil exécutif*, 1989, 42 p., publication des Nations Unies, numéro de vente: GV.F.89.0.7.

No. 6 -   *Bibliographical Survey of Secondary Literature on Military Expenditures*, November 1989, 39 p. United Nations publication, Sales No. GV.E.89.0.14.

No. 7 -   *Science and Technology: Between Civilian and Military Research and Development - Armaments and development at variance*, by Marek Thee, November 1990, 23 p., United Nations publication, Sales No. GV.E.90.0.14.

No. 8 -   *Esquisse pour un nouveau paysage européen*, par Eric Remacle, octobre 1990, 178 p., publication des Nations Unies, numéro de vente GV.F.91.0.2.

No. 9 -   *The Third Review of the Biological Weapons Convention: Issues and Proposals*, by Jozef Goldblat and Thomas Bernauer, April 1991, 78 p., United Nations publication, Sales No. GV.E.91.0.5.

No. 10 - *Disarmament, Environment, and Development and their Relevance to the Least Developed Countries*, by Arthur H. Westing, October 1991, 108 p., United Nations publication, Sales No. GV.E.91.0.19.

No. 11 - *The Implications of IAEA Inspections under Security Council Resolution 687*, by Eric Chauvistré, February 1992, 72 p., United Nations publication, Sales No. GV.E.92.0.6.

No. 12 - *La Résolution 687 (3 avril 1991) du Conseil de sécurité dans l'affaire du Golfe : Problèmes de rétablissement et de garantie de la paix*, par Serge Sur, 1992, 65 p., publication des Nations Unies (**forthcoming**)

No. 13 - *Les mesures de confiance de la CSCE : documents et commentaires, d'Helsinki (1975) à Vienne (1990)*, publication des Nations Unies (**forthcoming**)

UNIDIR Newsletter
(quarterly)

Vol. 1,   No. 1, March/mars 1988, *Disarmament-Development/Désarmement-Développement*, 16 p.

No. 2, June/juin 1988, *Research in Africa/La recherche en Afrique*, 28 p.

No. 3, September/septembre 1988, *Conventional Armaments Limitation and CBMs in Europe/Limitation des armements classiques et mesures de confiance en Europe*, 32 p.

No. 4, December/décembre 1988, *Research in Asia and the Pacific/La recherche en Asie et dans le Pacifique*, 40 p.

Vol. 2,   No. 1, March/mars 1989, *Chemical Weapons: Research Projects and Publications/Armes chimiques: projets de recherche et publications*, 24 p.

No. 2, June/juin 1989, *Research in Latin America and the Caribbean/La recherche en Amérique Latine et dans les Caraïbes*, 32 p.

No. 3, September/septembre 1989, *Outer Space/L'espace extra-atmosphérique*, 32 p.

No. 4, December/Décembre 1989, *Research in Eastern Europe/La recherche en Europe de l'Est*, 48p.

Vol. 3,   No. 1, March/mars 1990, *Verification of Disarmament Agreements/La vérification des accords sur le désarmement*, 48 p.

No. 2, June/juin 1990, *Research in North America/La recherche en Amérique du Nord*, 72 p.

No. 3, September/septembre 1990, *Nuclear Non-Proliferation/La non-prolifération nucléaire*, 43 p.

No. 4, December/décembre 1990, *Research in Western and Northern Europe (I)/ La recherche en Europe de l'Ouest et en Europe du Nord (I)*, 72 p.

Vol. 4,   No. 1, March/mars 1991, *Research in Western and Northern Europe (II) / La recherche en Europe de l'Ouest et en Europe du Nord (II)*, 72 p.

No. 2, June/juin 1991, *Biological Weapons / Armes biologiques*, 40 p.

No. 3, September/septembre 1991, *Naval and Maritime Issues/Questions navales et maritimes*, 54 p.

No. 4, December/décembre 1991, *Bilateral (US-USSR) Agreements and Negotiations / Accords et négociations bilatéraux (EU-URSS)*, 52 p.

Vol. 5,   No. 1, March-April/mars-avril 1992, *Conference on Disarmament / La Conférence du Désarmement*